1 Workbook

Pippa and Pop

T0306633

American English

Colin Sage

with Caroline Nixon & Michael Tomlinson

CAMBRIDGE UNIVERSITY PRESS

Map of the book

	VOCABULARY	LANGUAGE	SOUNDS AND LETTERS	LITERACY AND VALUE	NUMBERS	CROSS-CURRICULAR
Introduction Page 4						
1 My friends Page 6	*Hello* *Pippa, Pop, Dan, Kim* *book, crayon, pencil*	*Hello. I'm (Pippa).* *What's this?* *It's a (pencil).*	Distinguishing sounds	*Duck's friend* Be friendly	Numbers: *1, 2*	Social studies: Sharing
2 My family Page 18	*brother, sister,* *daddy, mommy* *boy, girl, man, woman*	*She's the (mommy).* *He's my (brother).* *He's / She's a (boy).*	Distinguishing sounds	*The big carrot* Help your family	Numbers: *3, 4*	Science: How food grows
3 My toys Page 30	*ball, doll, teddy bear, train* *blue, brown, red, yellow*	*It's a (ball).* *It's (red).*	Distinguishing between letters and objects	*Big teddy bear, small teddy bear* Celebrate differences	Recognizing patterns	Math: Big and small
Units 1–3 Review Pages 42–43						
4 My body Page 44	*ears, eyes, mouth, nose* *arms, feet, hands, legs*	*Touch your (nose).* *Color the (arms).*	Distinguishing between letters and numbers	*Bunny's family* Be kind	Recognizing patterns	Social studies: Feelings

	VOCABULARY	LANGUAGE	SOUNDS AND LETTERS	LITERACY AND VALUE	NUMBERS	CROSS-CURRICULAR
5 **Food** Page 56	*apples, bananas, cookies, sandwiches* *juice, milk, water*	*I like (apples).* *I don't like (juice).*	The letter sound *a*	*Picky Peter* *Say thank you*	Numbers: *5, 6*	Science: Identifying fruit
6 **Animals** Page 68	*cat, dog, fish, rabbit* *chair, table; on, under*	*Where's the (cat)? Here it is.* *It's (under) the (chair).*	The letter sound *e*	*Emma's new cat* Be kind to animals	Numbers: *7, 8*	Science: What animals need
Units 4–6 Review Pages 80–81						
7 **Clothes** Page 82	*hat, jacket, shoes, socks* *dress, pants, skirt, T-shirt*	*(Put on / Take off) your (hat).* *I have (a dress).*	The letter sound *i*	*Tommy's T-shirt* Be considerate	Shapes: *circle, square, triangle*	Art: Rough and smooth
8 **Transportation** Page 94	*bike, bus, car, van* *drive a car, jump, ride a bike, run*	*I can see a (car).* *I can (ride a bike).*	The letter sound *o*	*The hare and the tortoise* Be careful	Numbers: *9, 10*	Science: Fast and slow
9 **The park** Page 106	*bird, flower, frog, tree; green, pink* *butterflies, caterpillars, ladybugs, worms*	*A (green) (tree).* *What are these? They're (butterflies).*	The letter sound *u*	*Penny in the park* Take care of nature	One more	Math: Symmetry
Units 7–9 Review Pages 118–119						

Welcome

Look. Find. Color.

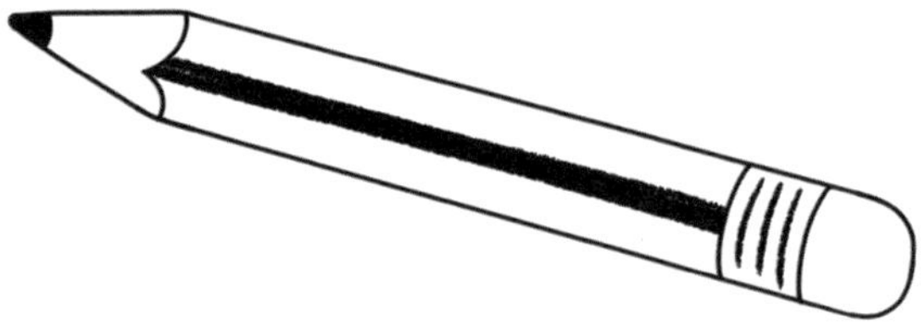
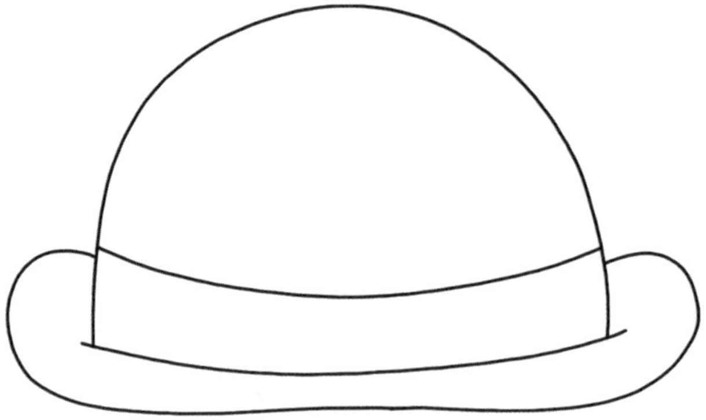

Look. Find. Trace. Say.

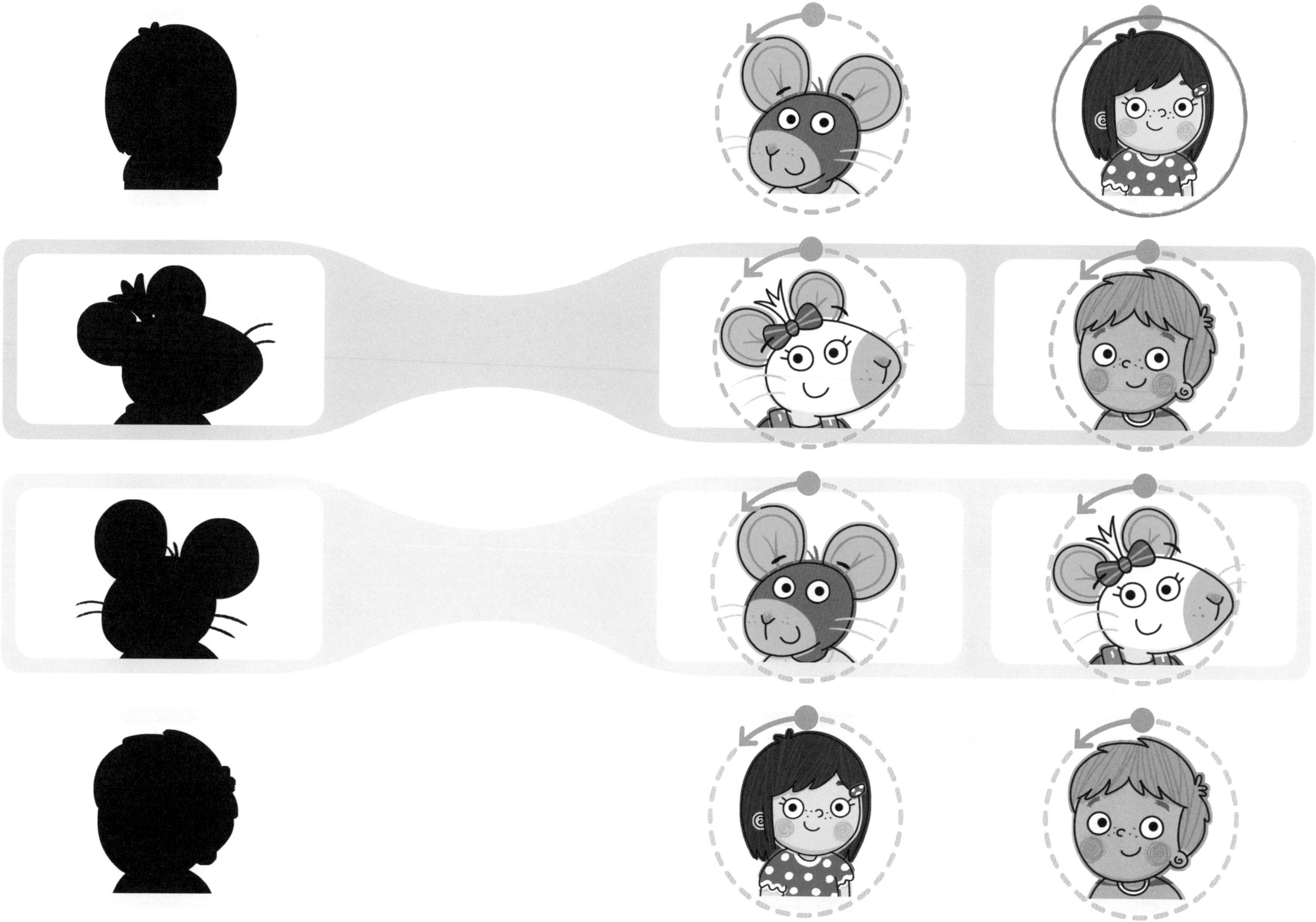

1 My friends

Listen again. Look. Stick. Point.

Look. Trace. Say.

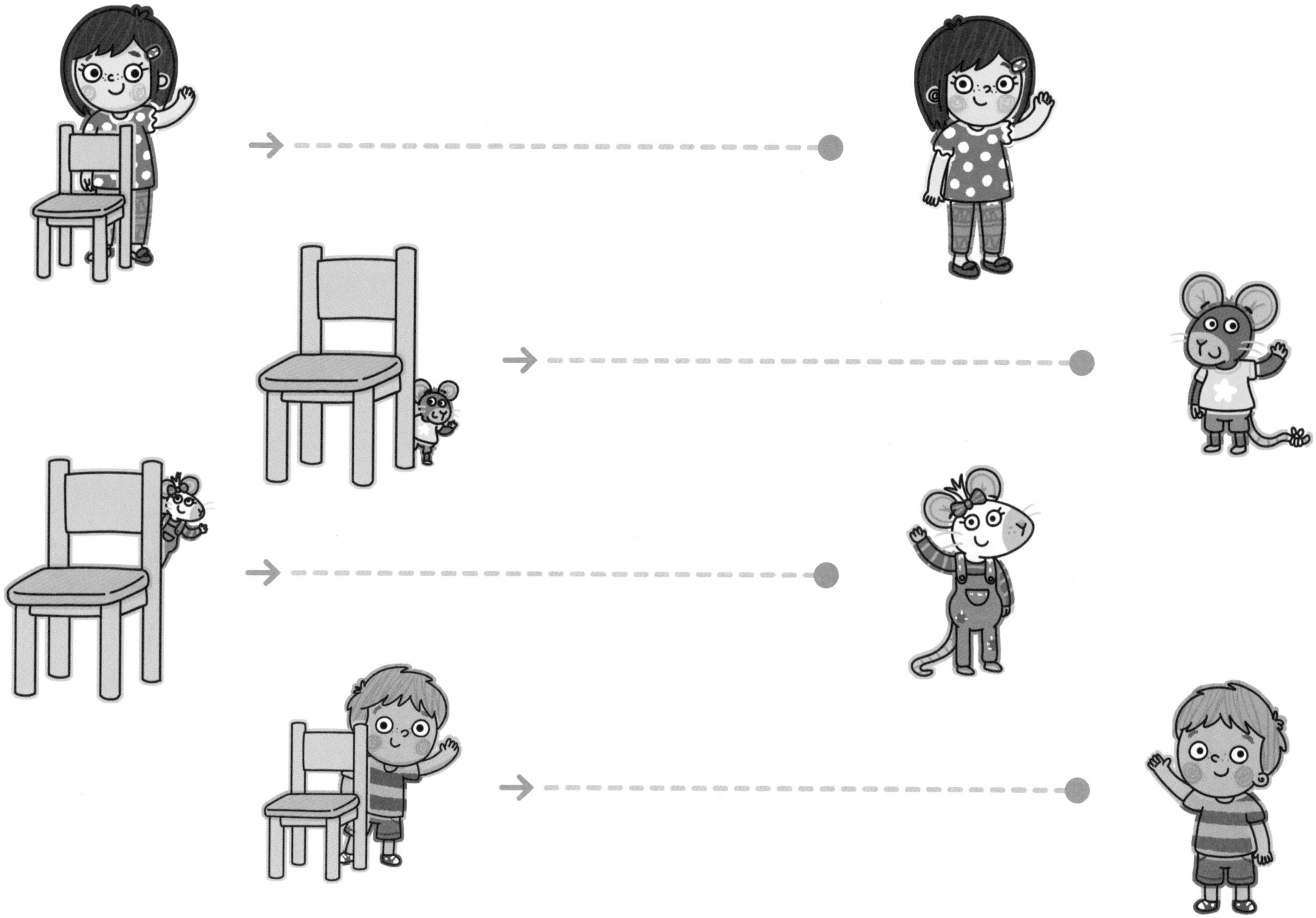

At home Point to Kim, Pop, Pippa and Dan.

Look. Find. Trace. Say.

1 **Language practice:** *Hello. I'm (Pippa / Pop / Dan / Kim).*

6 **Listen again. Look. Trace.**

Look. Point. Trace.

Look. Find. Color.

At home

How are you friendly?

Look. Trace. Color. Say.

Look. Find. Color. Say.

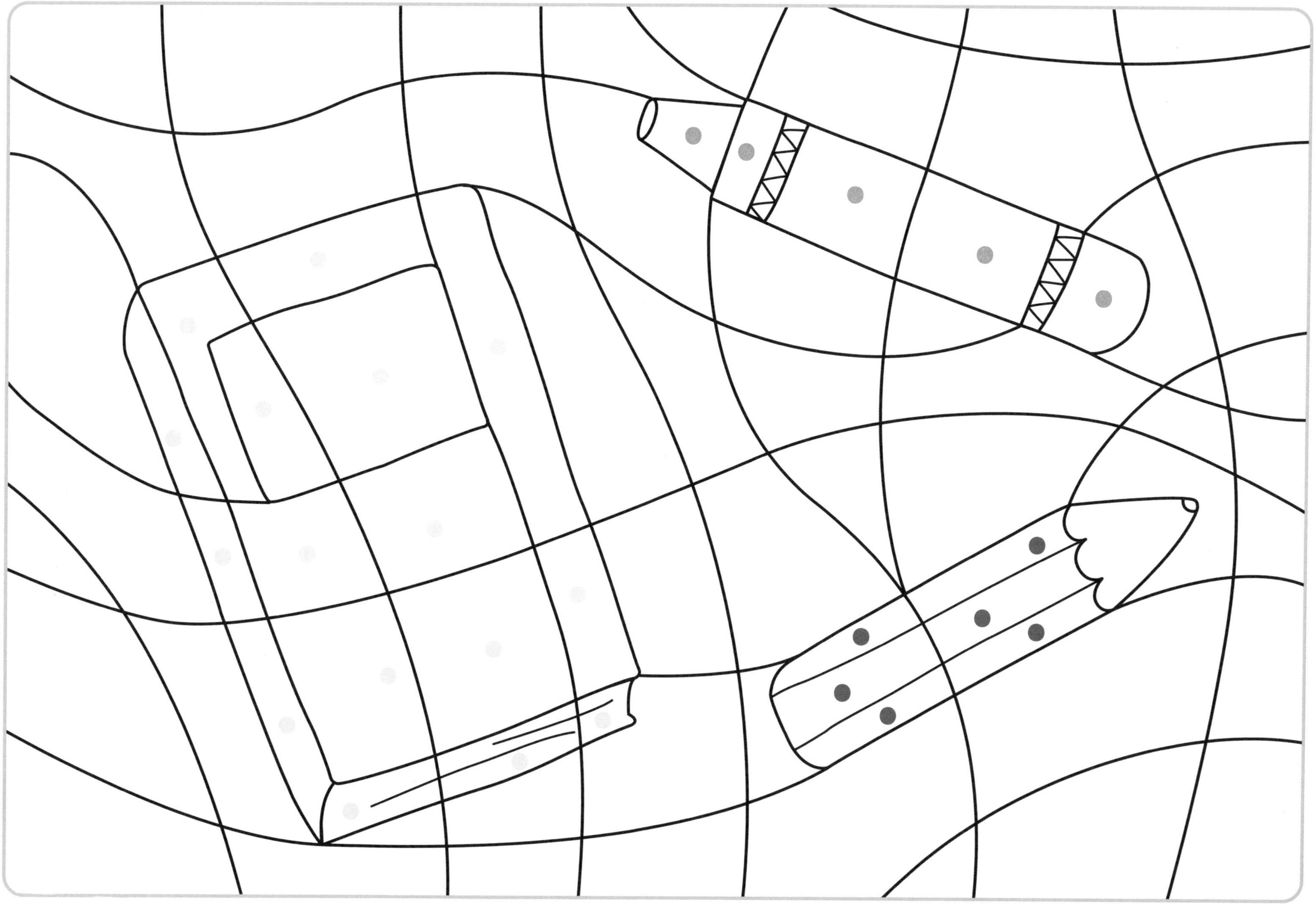

Look. Count. Trace. Say.

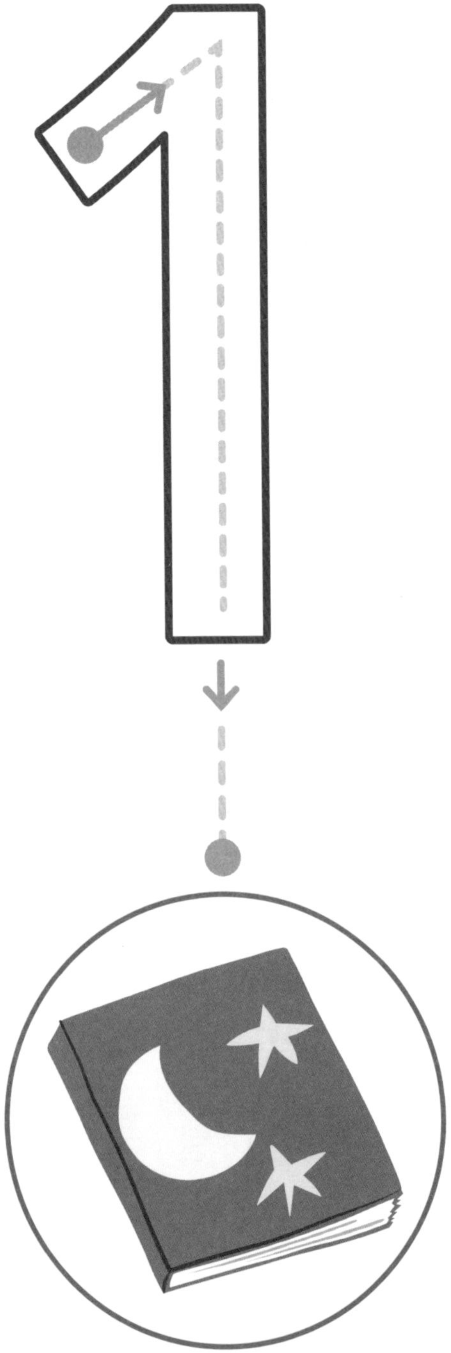

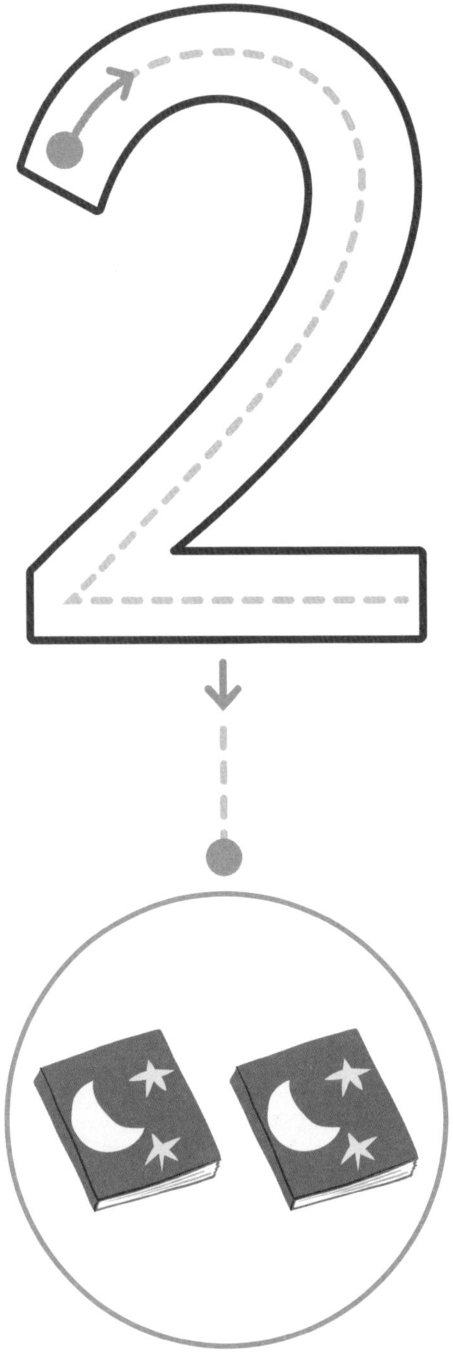

Look. Find. Color.

Look. Draw. Say.

At home Talk to a friend. Say *Hello. I'm (Anna).*

Point. Say. Color.

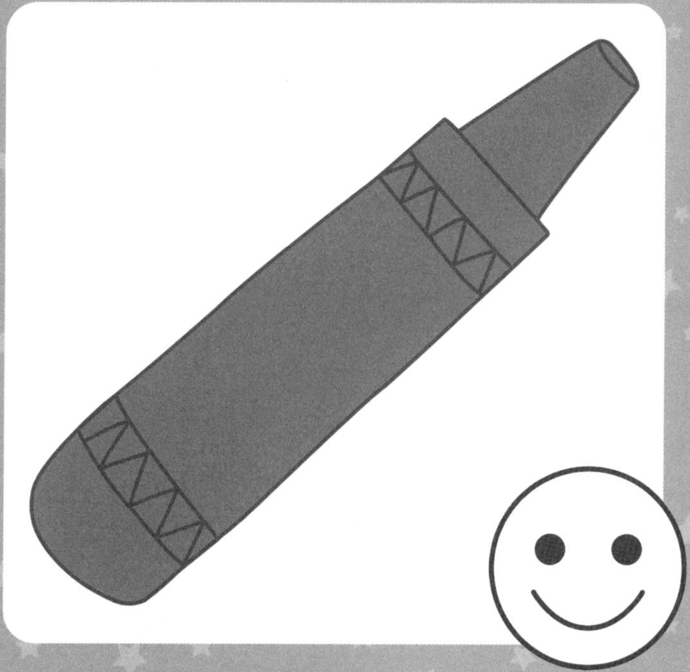

2 My family

11 **Listen again.** **Look.** **Stick.** **Point.**

Look. Color. Say.

Look. Find. Trace. Say.

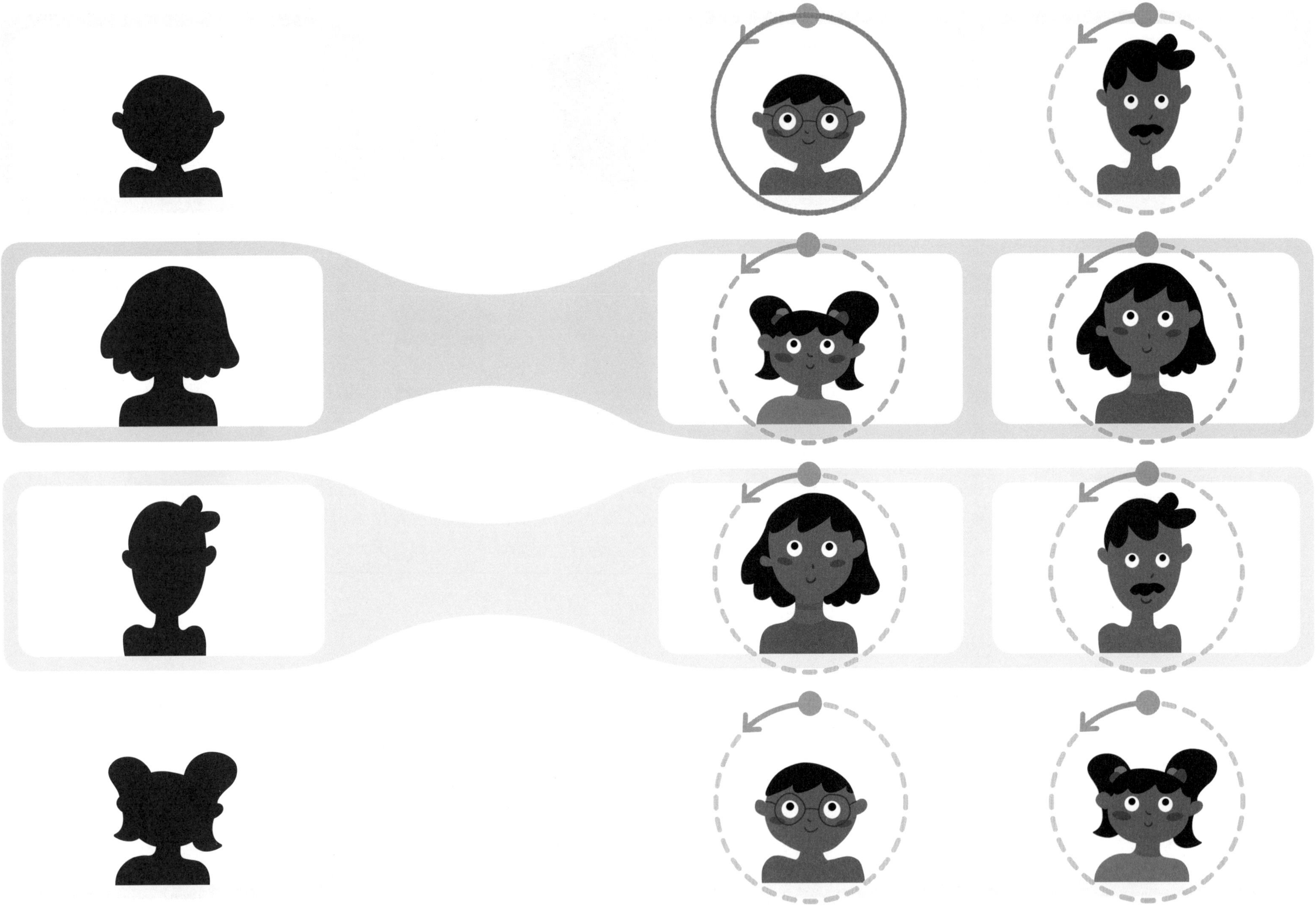

At home Find a picture of your family. Point and say.

 2 **Language practice:** *He's the (daddy / brother). She's the (mommy / sister).*

14 **Listen again. Look. Trace.**

Look. Point. Trace.

Look. Find. Color.

At home

Who do you help?

Look. Trace. Say.

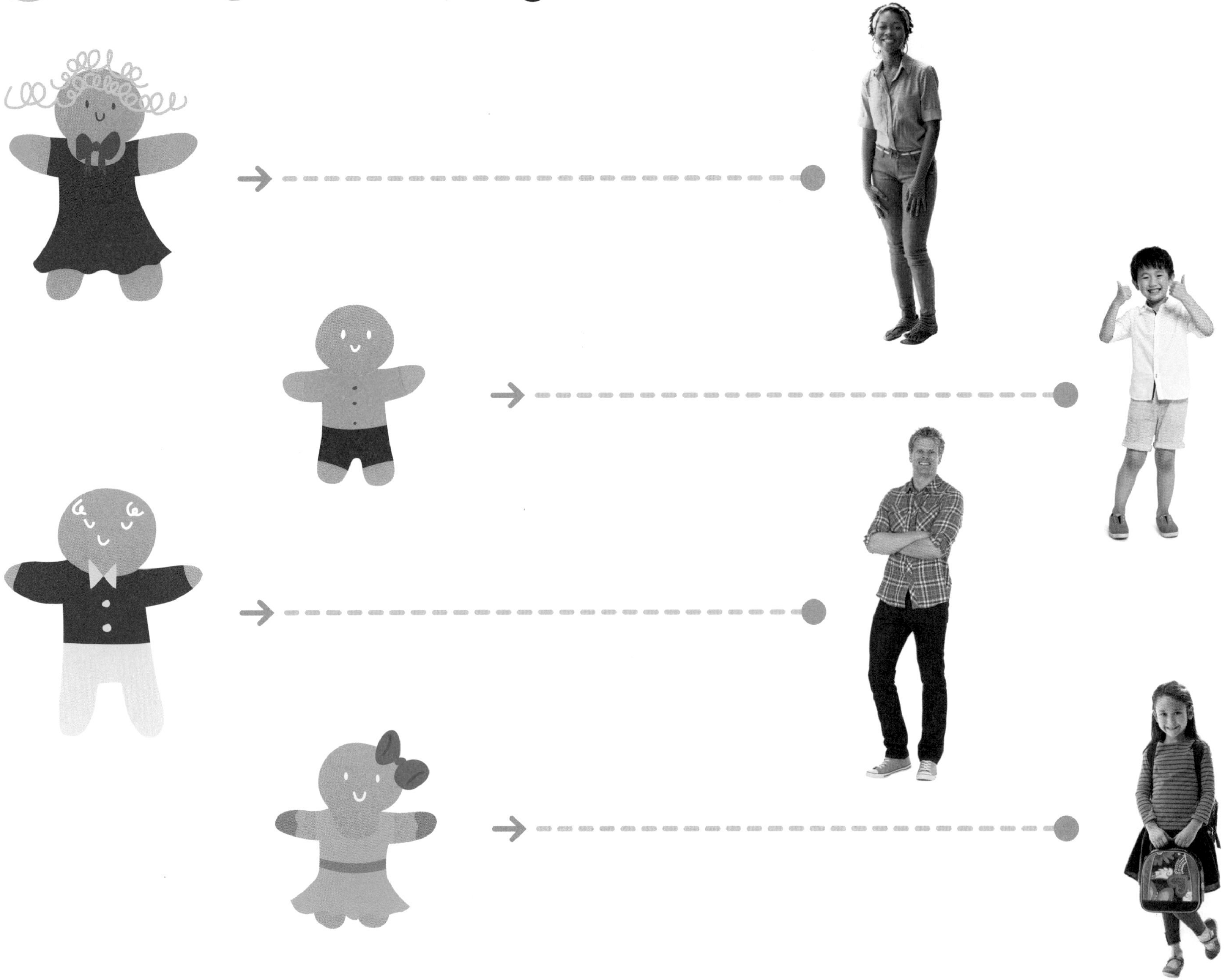

Look. Find. Trace. Say.

Look. Count. Trace. Say.

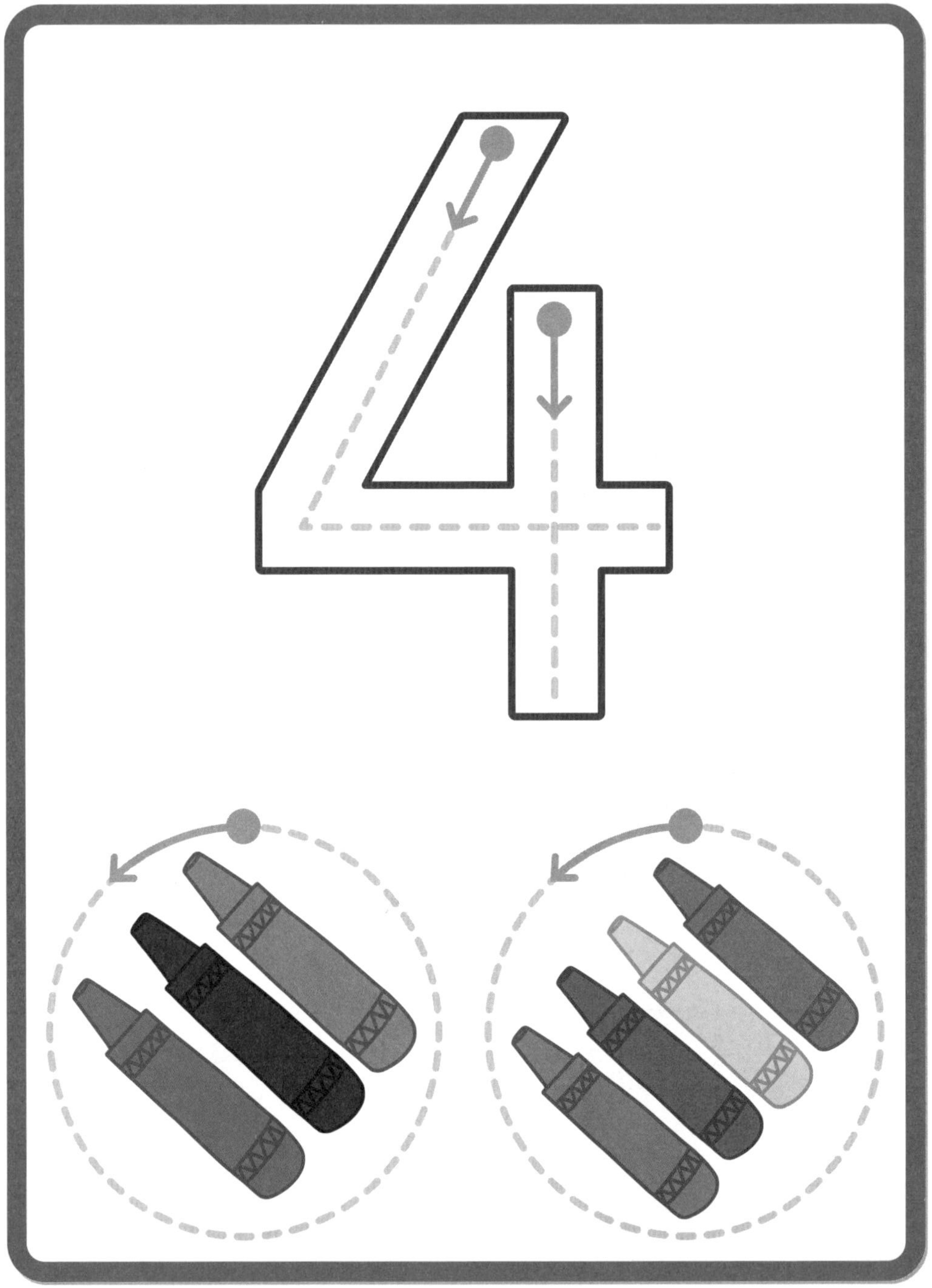

Look. Color. Say.

At home Look in the kitchen.
Where is the food from?

Look. Draw. Say.

2 *She's my (mommy / sister). He's my (daddy / brother).*

Point. Say. Color.

3 My toys

19 **Listen again.** **Look.** **Stick.** **Point.**

Look. Find. Color. Say.

At home Find a train, ball, teddy bear and doll. Say.

Look. Trace. Say.

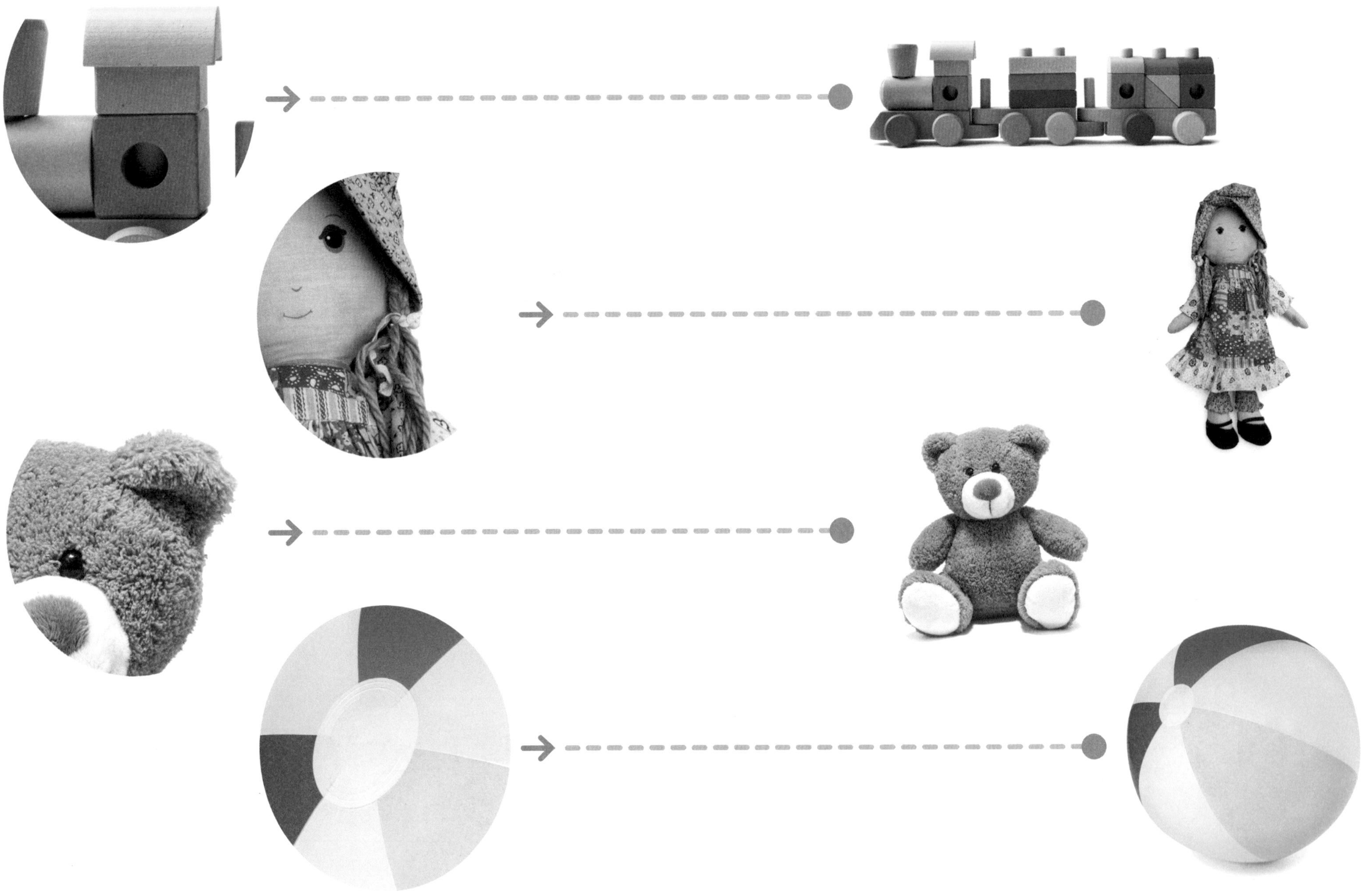

3 **Language practice:** *It's a (train / doll / teddy bear / ball).*

Point. Color.

a

t

g

b

Look. Point. Trace.

Draw. Color. Say.

At home

How are you different from your friends?

Look. Color. Say.

3 **Vocabulary practice:** *blue, red, yellow, brown*

Look. Color. Say.

Look. Color. Say.

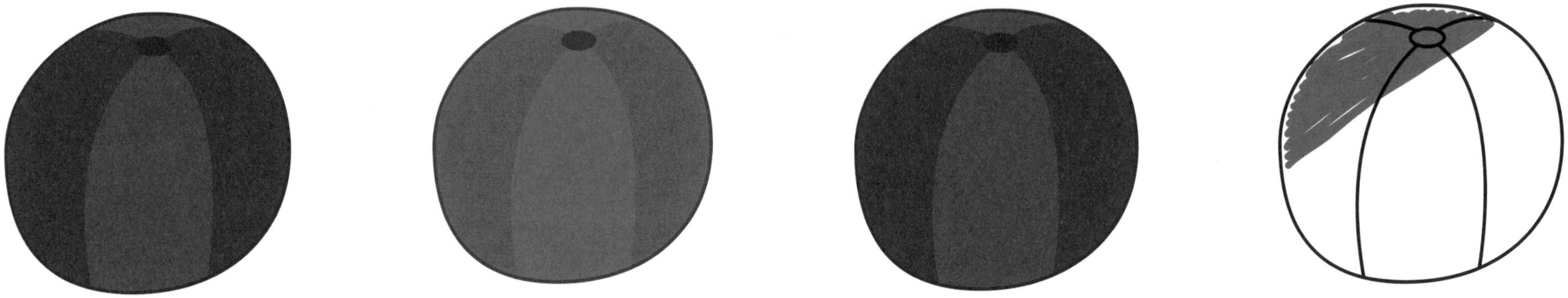

Look. Find. Color. Say.

At home

Find 2 big things
and 2 small things.

Look. Draw. Say.

3 *It's (yellow).*

Point. Say. Color.

It's a (train / teddy bear / doll / ball).

Look. Find. Color. Say.

Look. Count. Trace. Say.

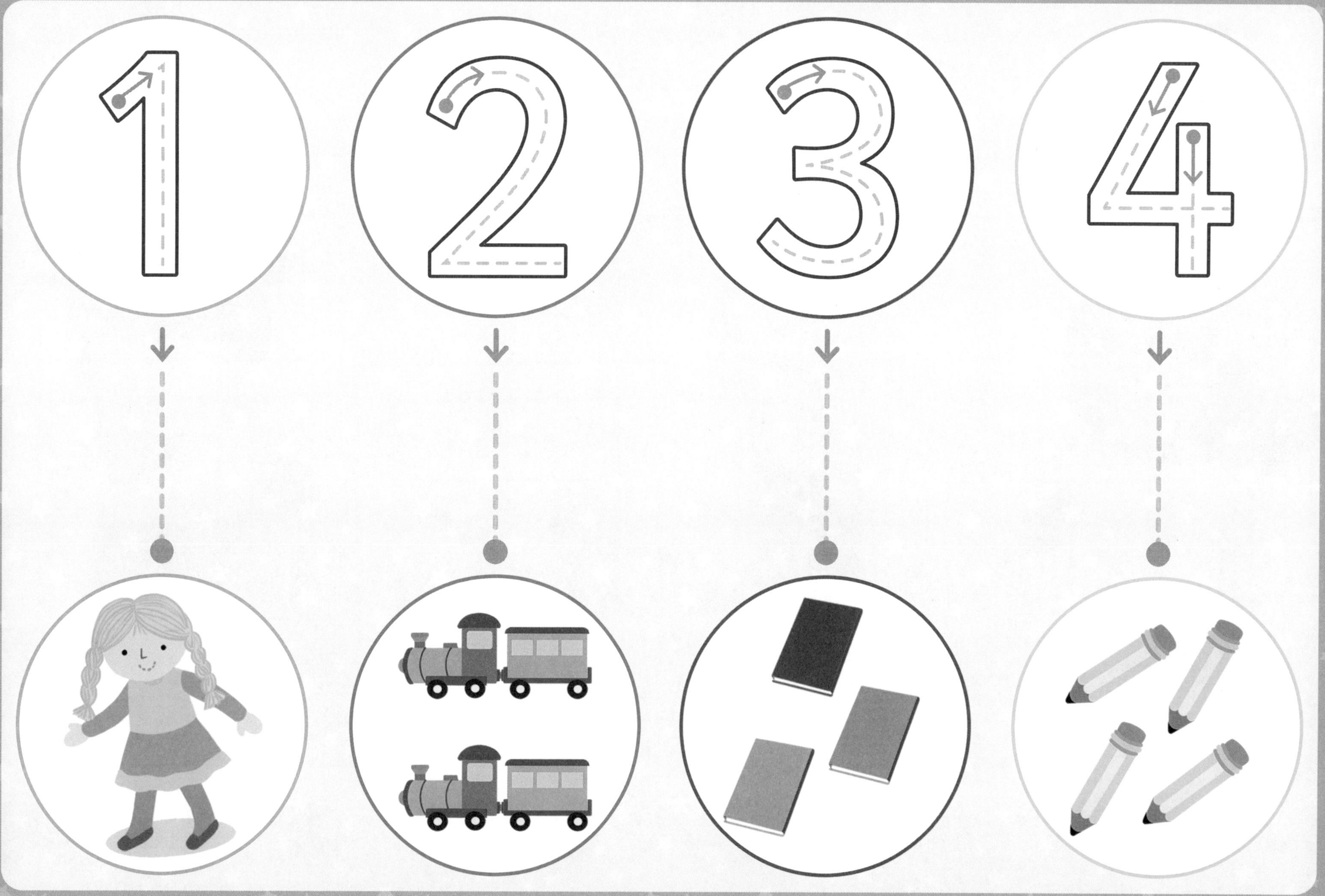

4 My body

27 Listen again. Look. Stick. Point.

Look. Find. Color. Say.

Look. Find. Trace. Say.

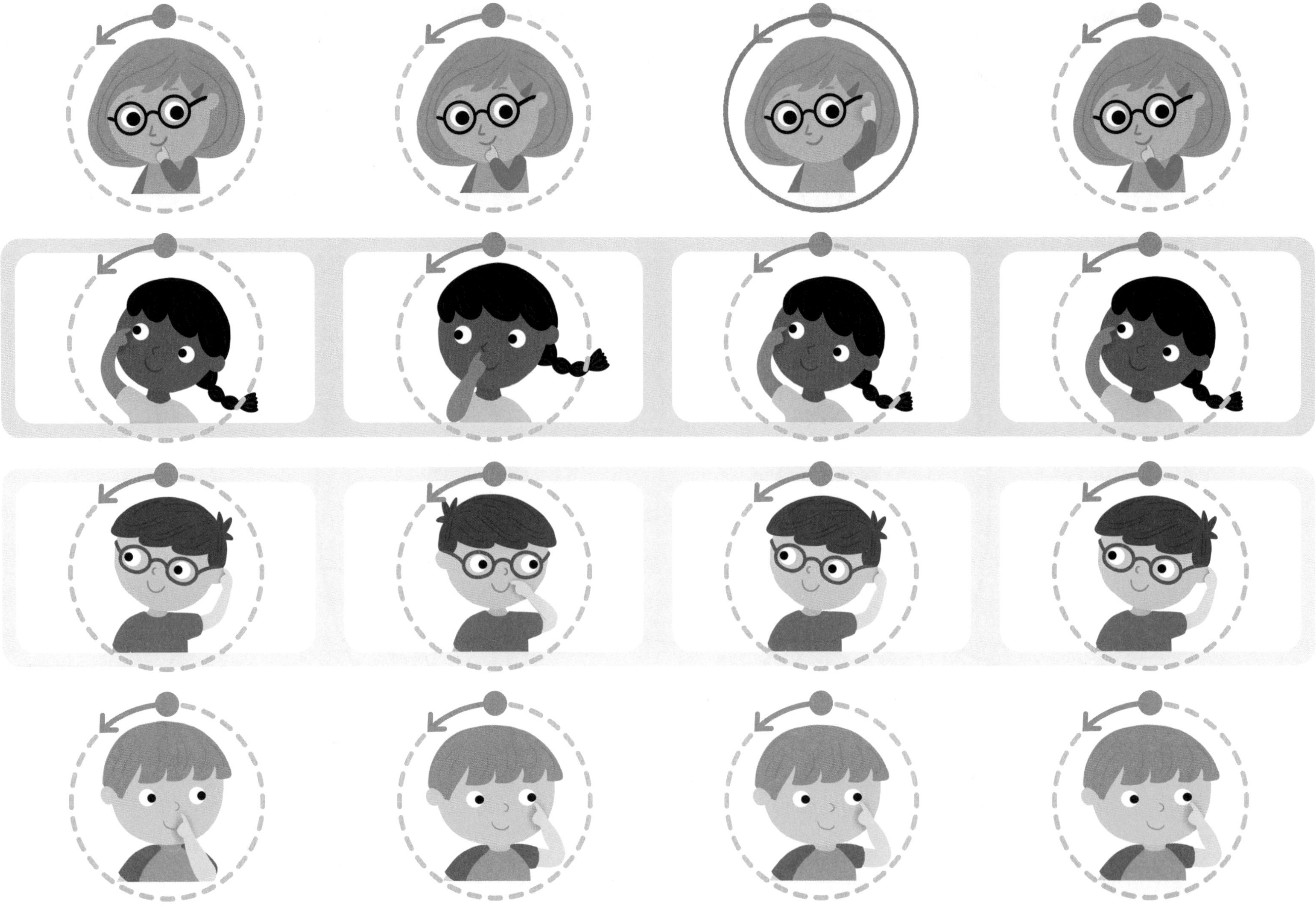

At home Touch your mouth, eyes, ears and nose. Say.

4 **Language practice:** *Touch your (mouth / eyes / ears / nose).*

Point. Color.

d 1 e 2

s 3 m 4

Look. Point. Trace.

Draw. Color. Say.

At home

How are you kind?

Look. Trace. Say.

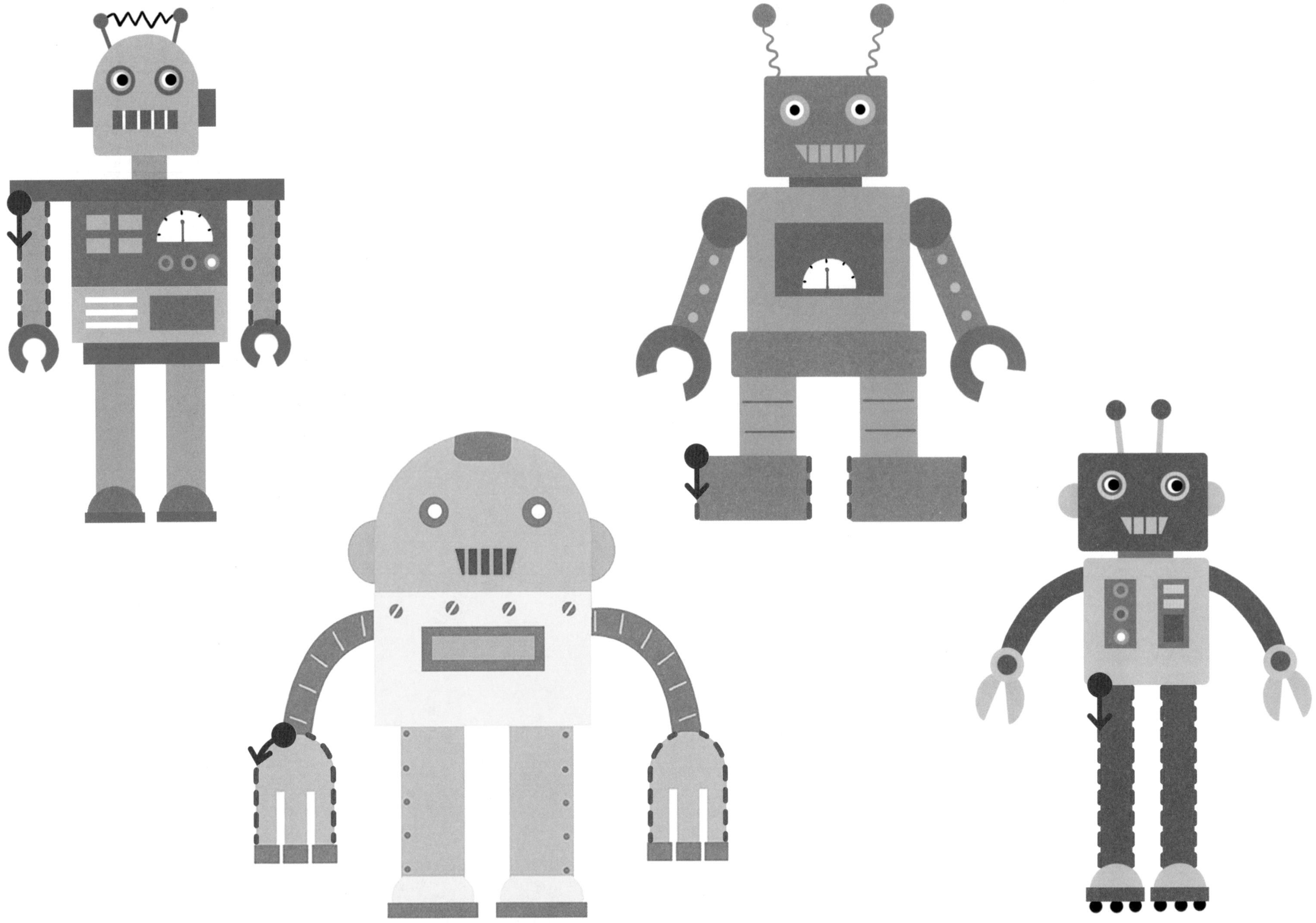

Look. Color. Say.

Look. Color. Say.

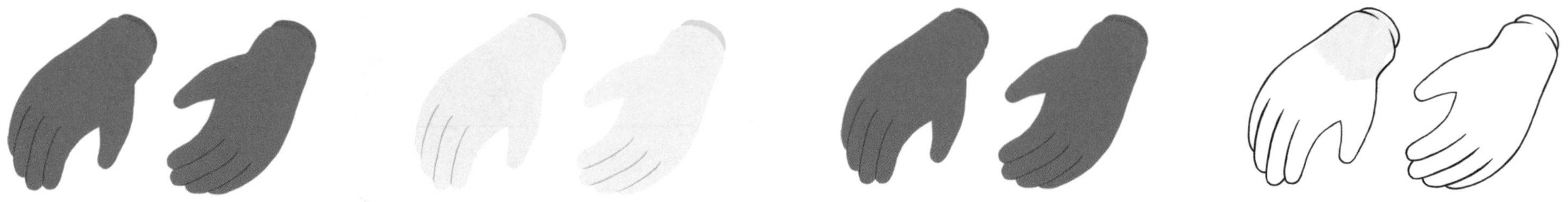

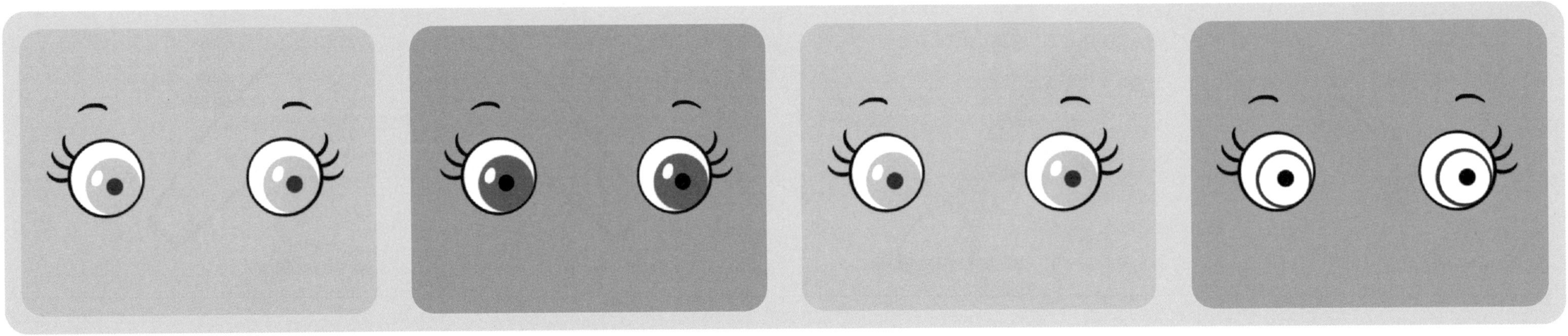

At home Make a pattern with toys.

Look. Find. Trace. Say.

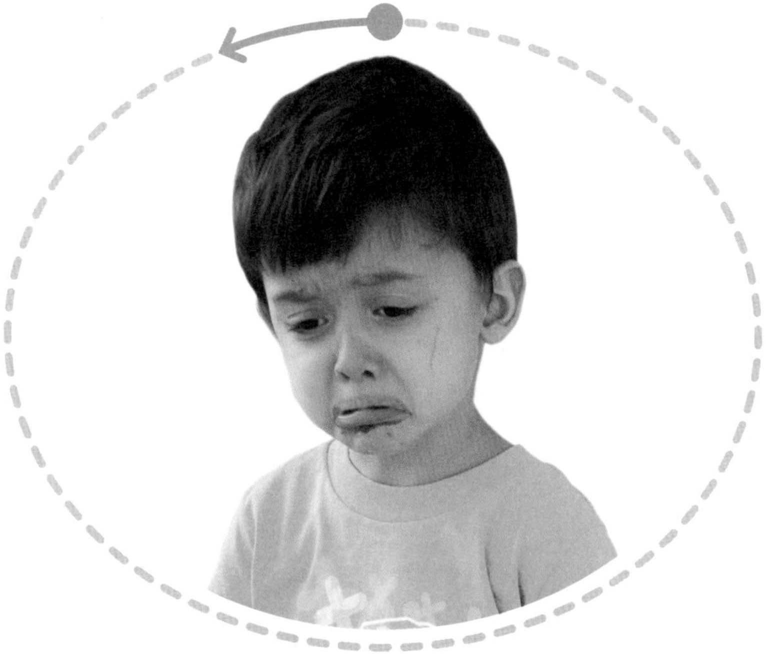

Look. Draw. Say.

4 *Touch your (ears / eyes / nose / mouth). Happy / Sad*

Point. Say. Color.

5 Food

36 **Listen again.** **Look.** **Stick.** **Point.**

Look. Find. Trace. Say.

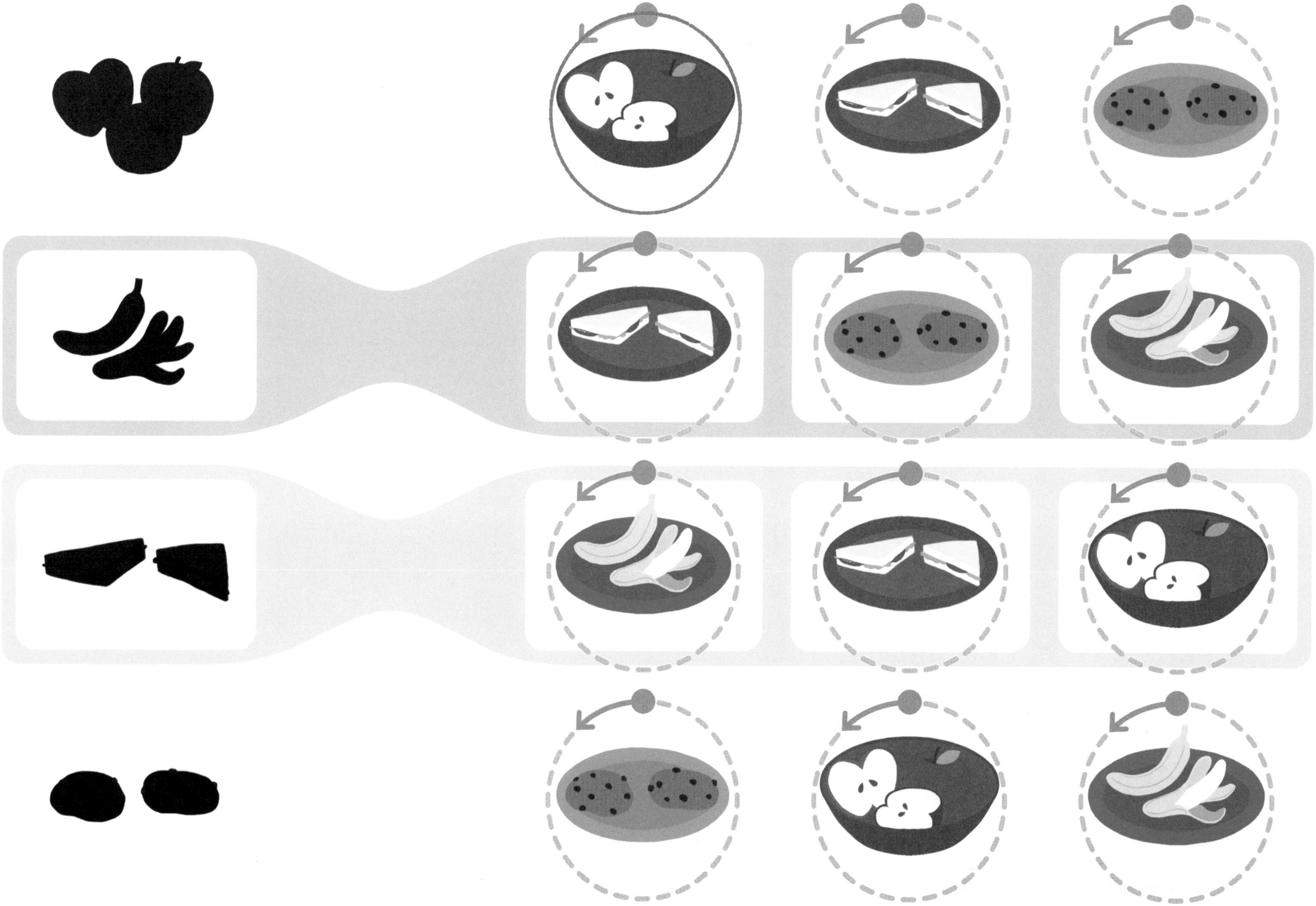

At home Look in a store. Find apples, bananas, sandwiches and cookies.

Look. Trace. Say.

5 **Language practice:** *I like (cookies / bananas / apples / sandwiches).*

39 **Listen again.** **Look.** **Find.** **Trace.** **Say.**

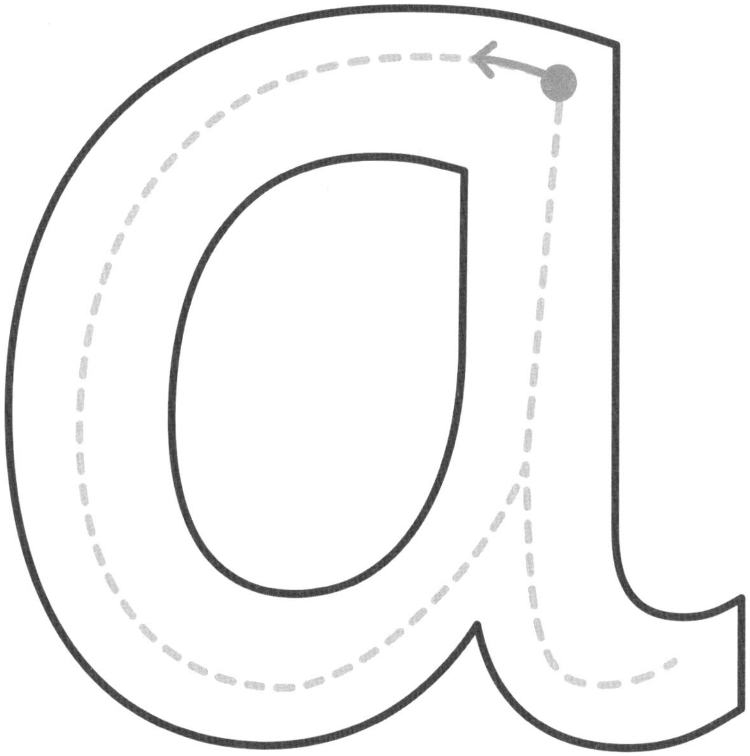

Look. Point. Trace.

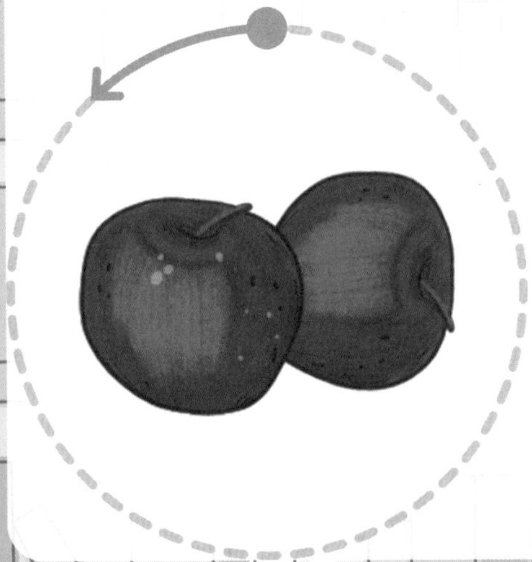

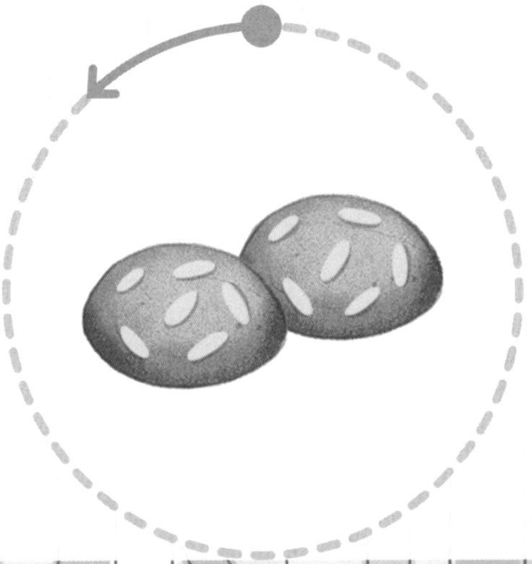

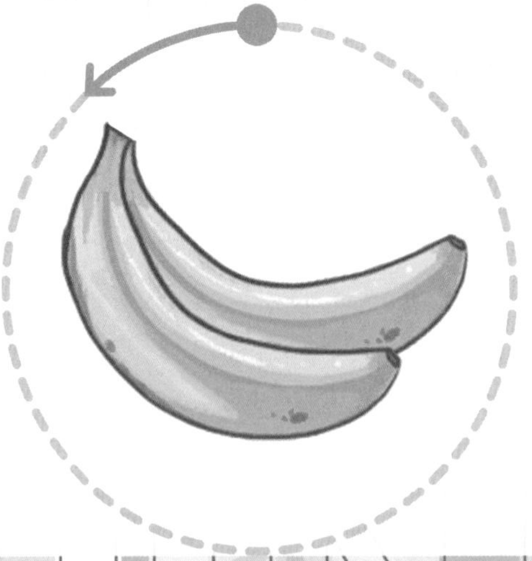

Look. Find. Color.

At home

Talk to your family.
Say *thank you*.

Look. Trace. Say.

Look. Color. Say.

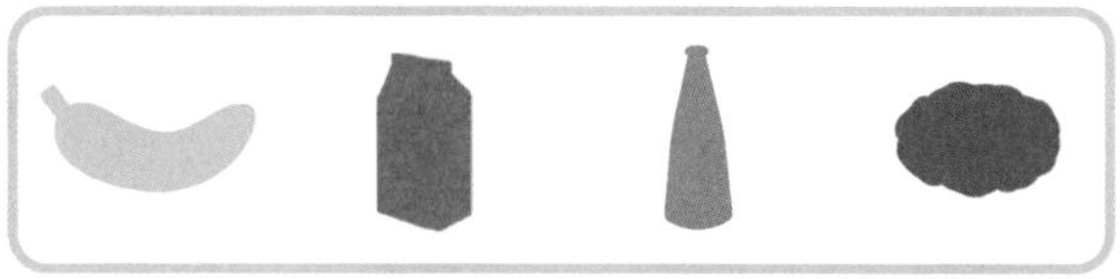

Look. Count. Trace. Say.

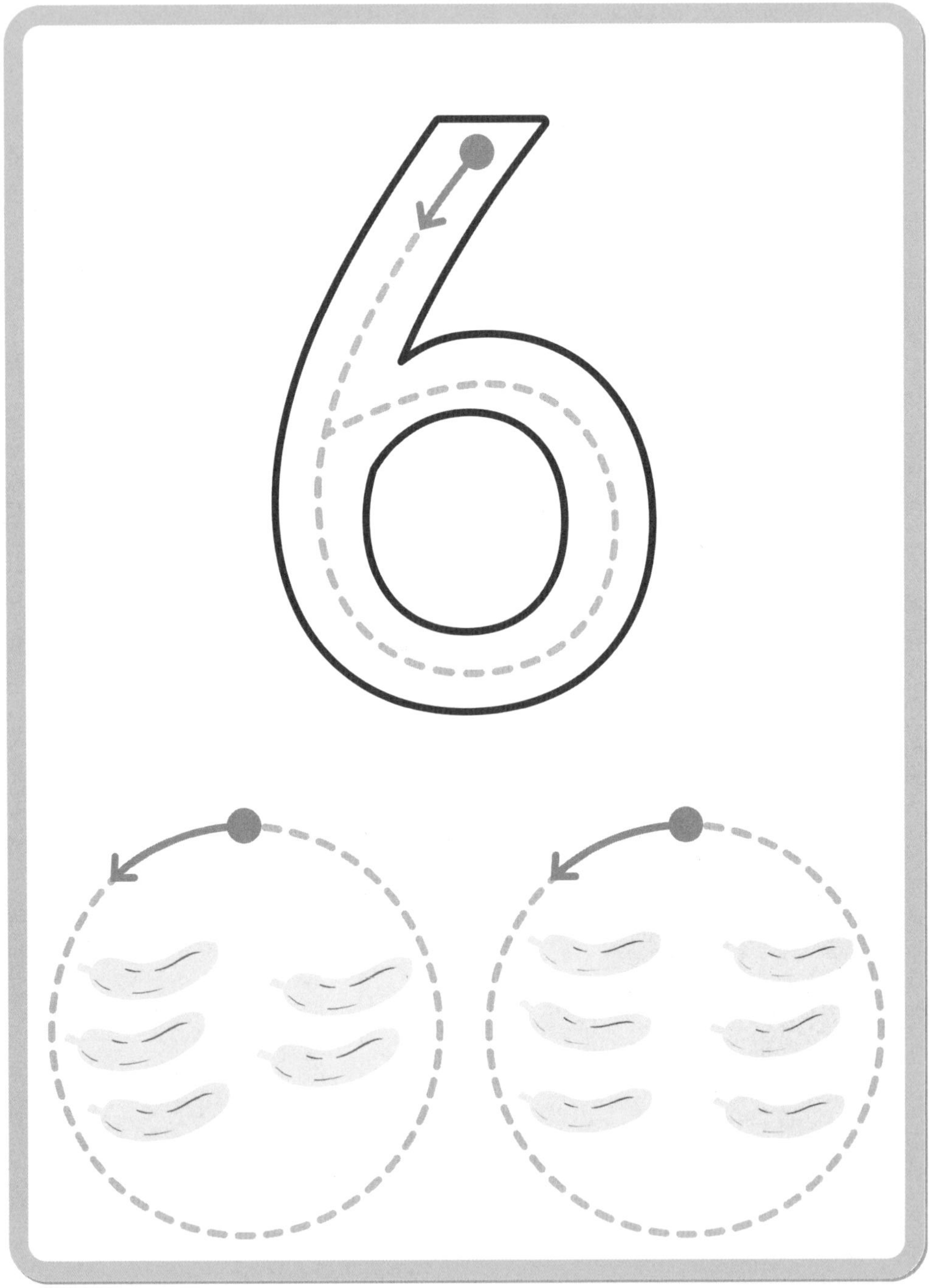

Look. Find. Color. Say.

At home

Look in the kitchen.
Point to the fruit.

Look. Draw. Say.

5 *I like (bananas).*

Point. Say. Color.

6 Animals

44 **Listen again. Look. Stick. Point.**

Look. Color. Count. Say.

At home

Do you like rabbits, dogs, cats and fish? Say.

Look. Trace. Say.

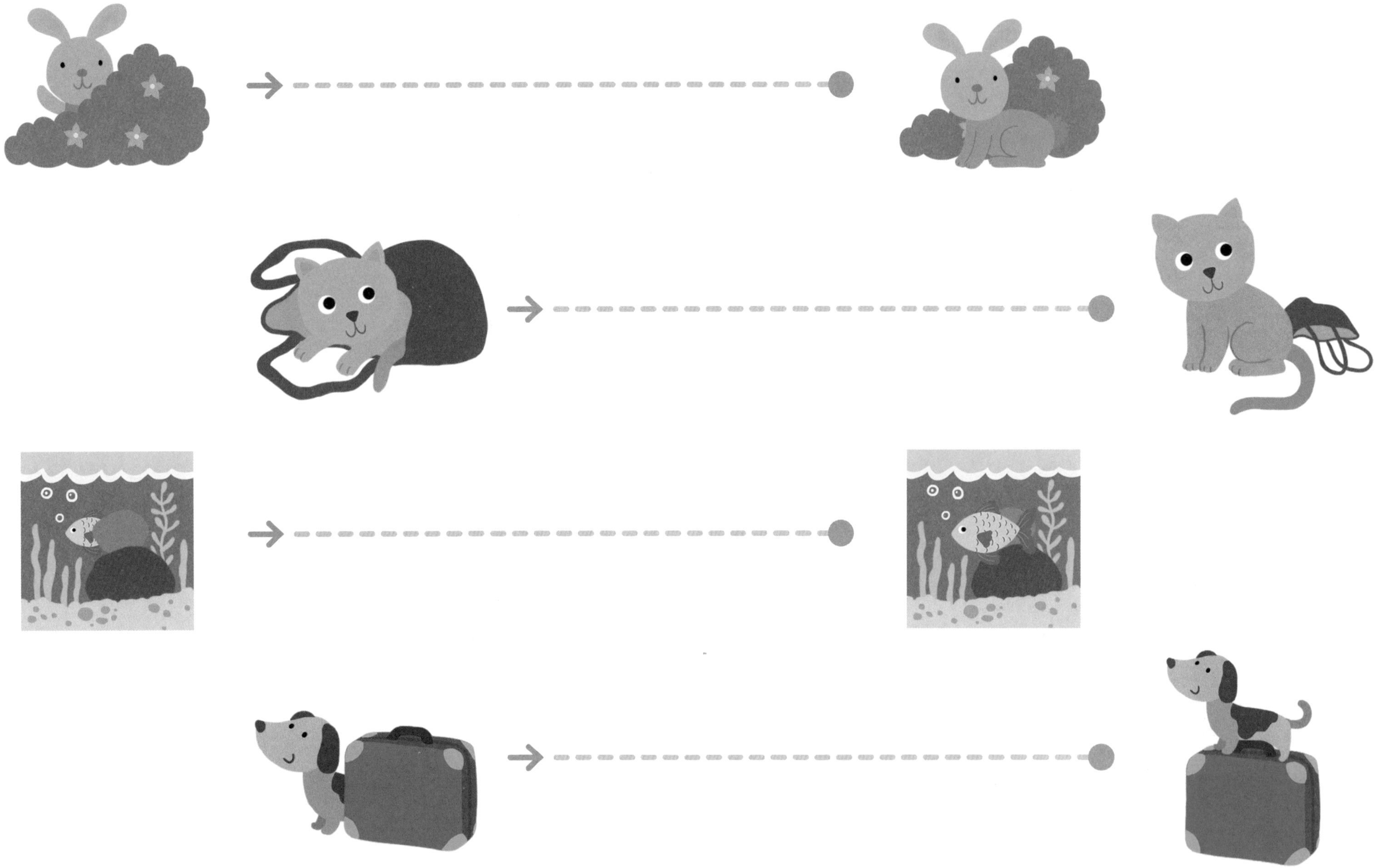

6 **Language practice:** *Where's the (rabbit / cat / fish / dog)? Here it is.*

47 **Listen again.** **Look.** **Find.** **Trace.** **Say.**

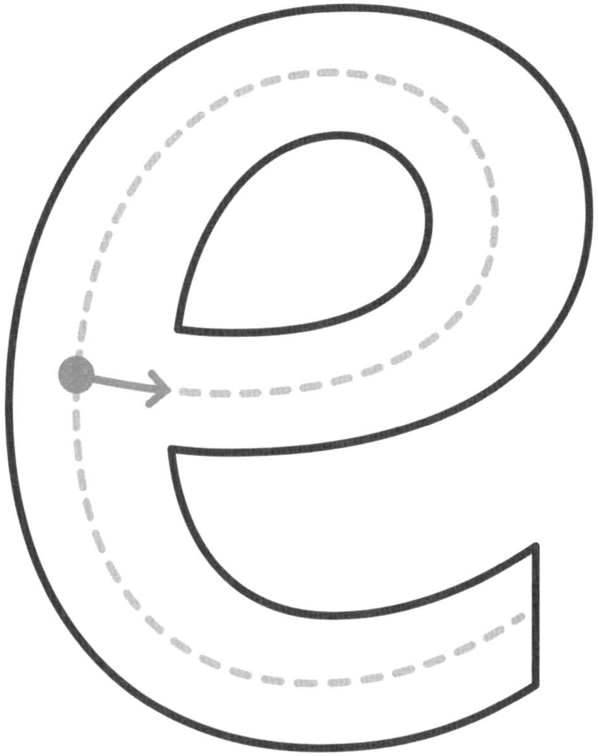

Look. Point. Trace.

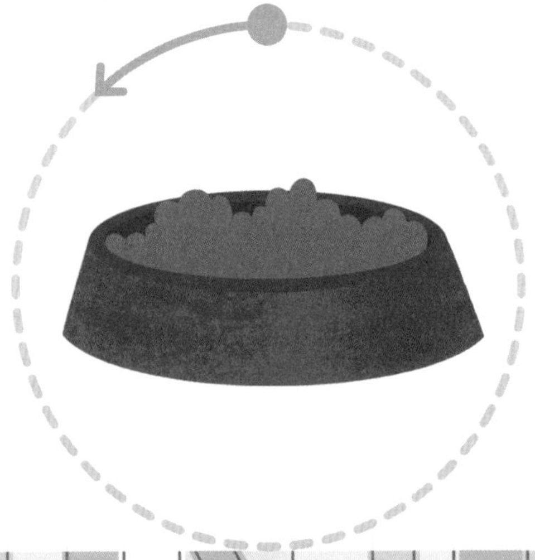

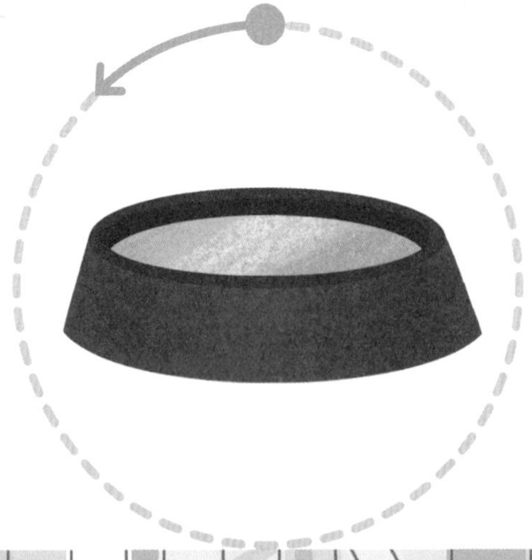

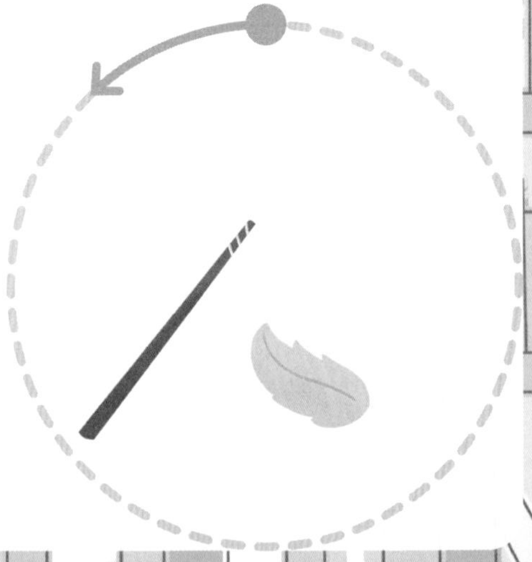

Look. Find. Color.

At home

How are you kind to animals?

Look. Find. Trace. Say.

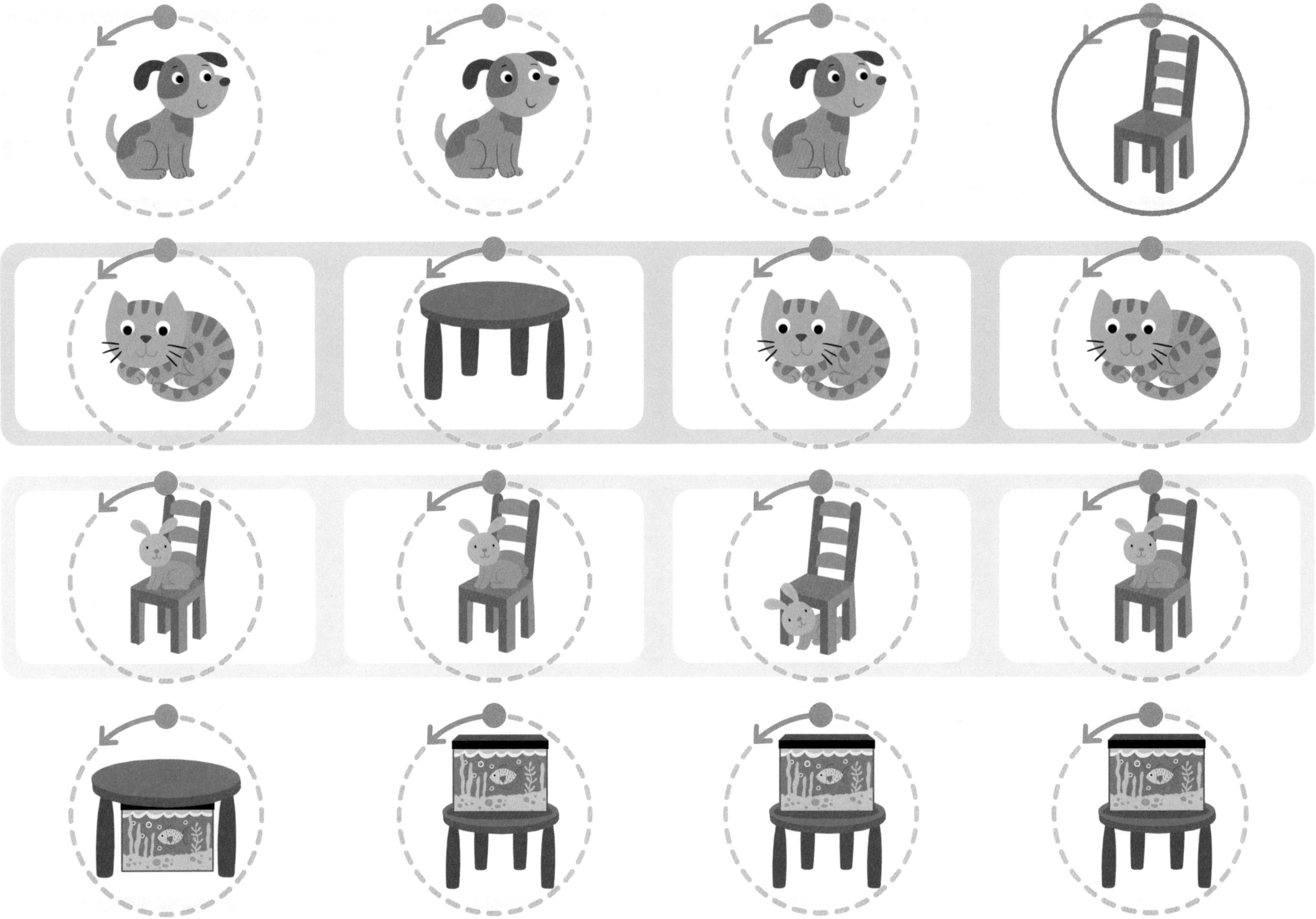

6 **Vocabulary practice:** *chair, table; on, under*

Look. Find. Circle. Say.

Look. Count. Trace. Say.

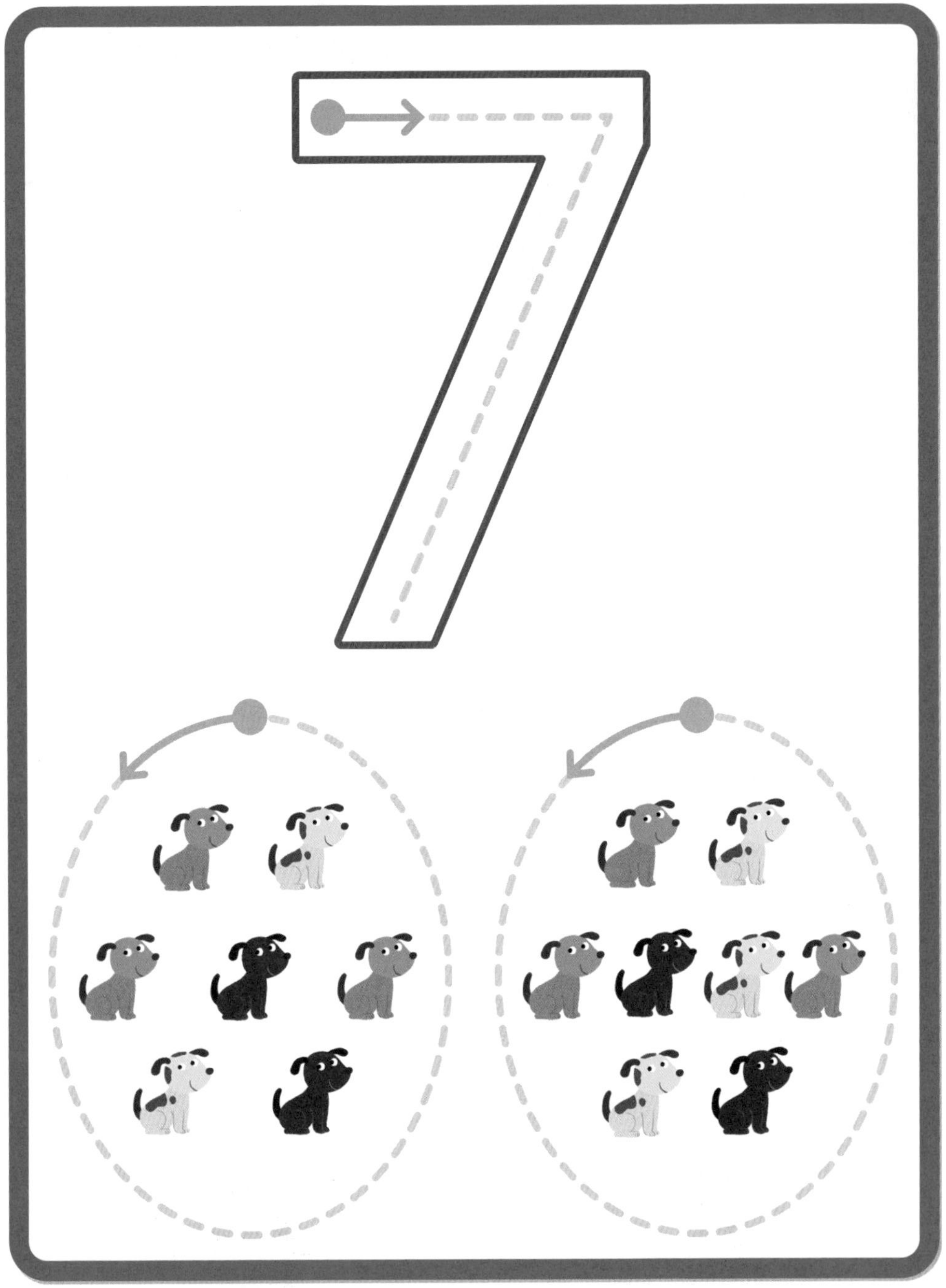

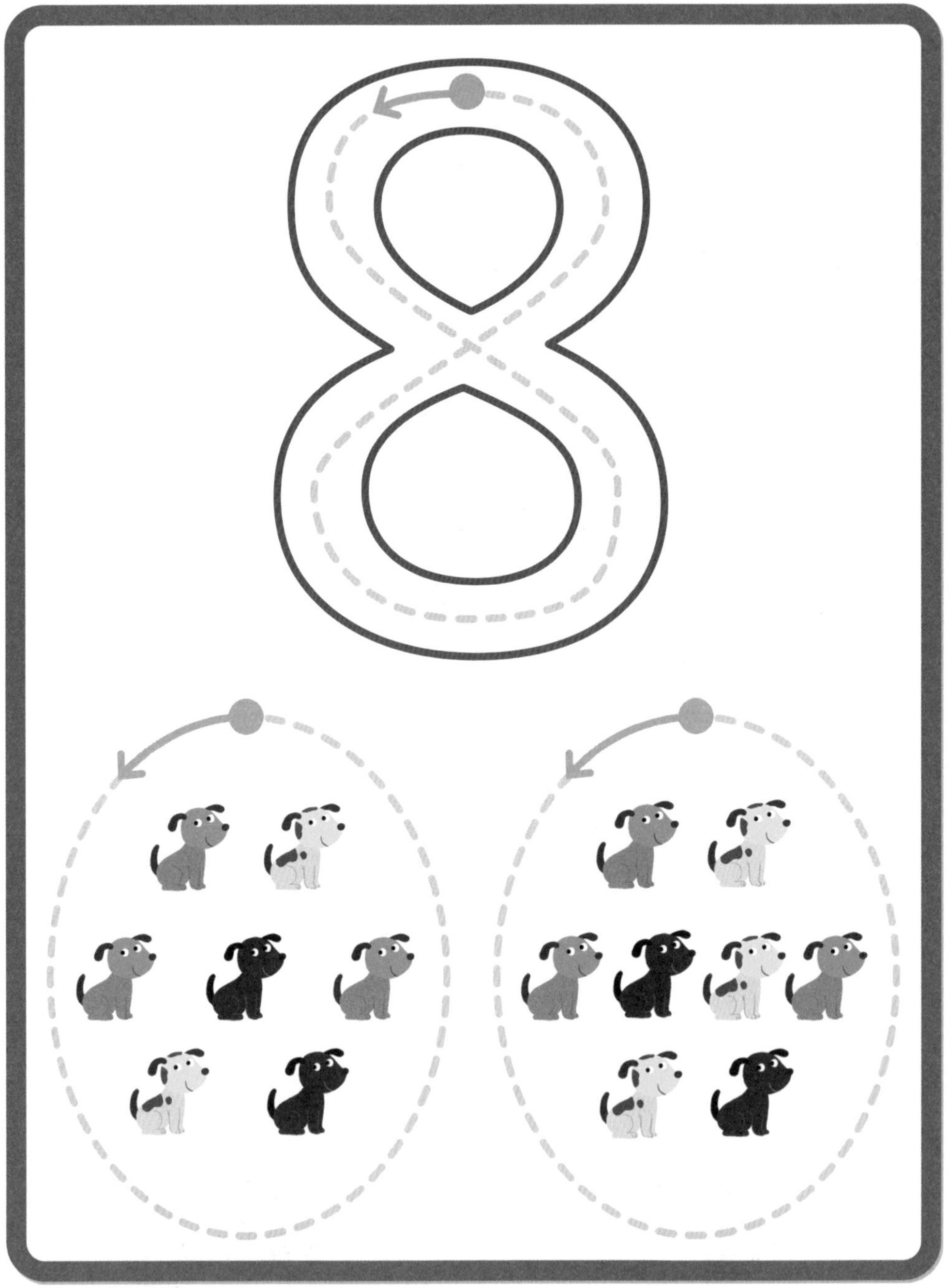

At home Find a toy animal.

Look. Find. Color.

Look. Draw. Say.

6 *Where's the (dog)? Here it is.*

Point. Say. Color.

Where's the (rabbit / dog / cat / fish)? It's (on / under) the (chair/ table).

Look. Find. Color. Say.

Look. Count. Trace. Say.

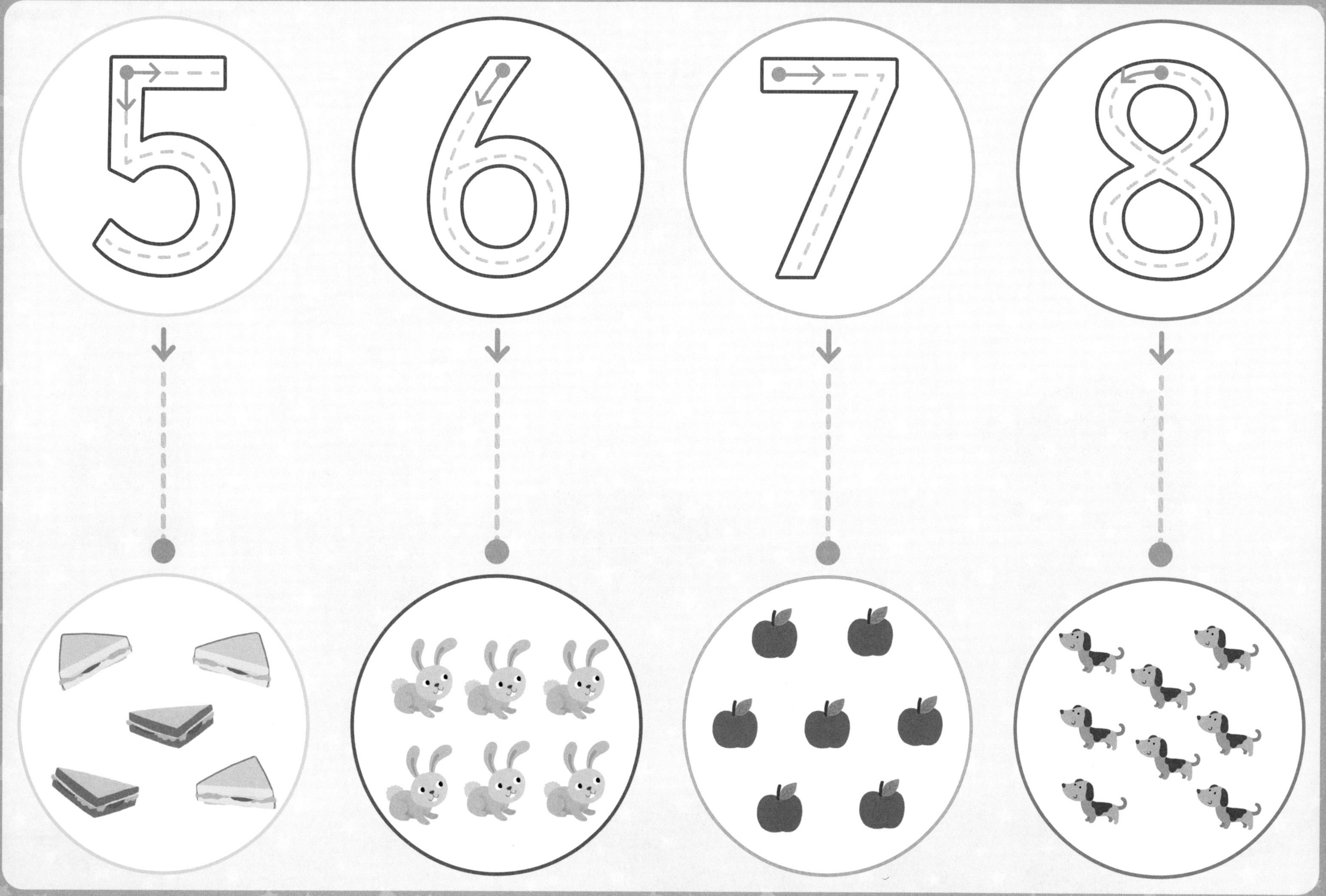

7 Clothes

53 Listen again. Look. Stick. Point.

Look. Find. Circle. Say.

Look. Find. Trace. Say.

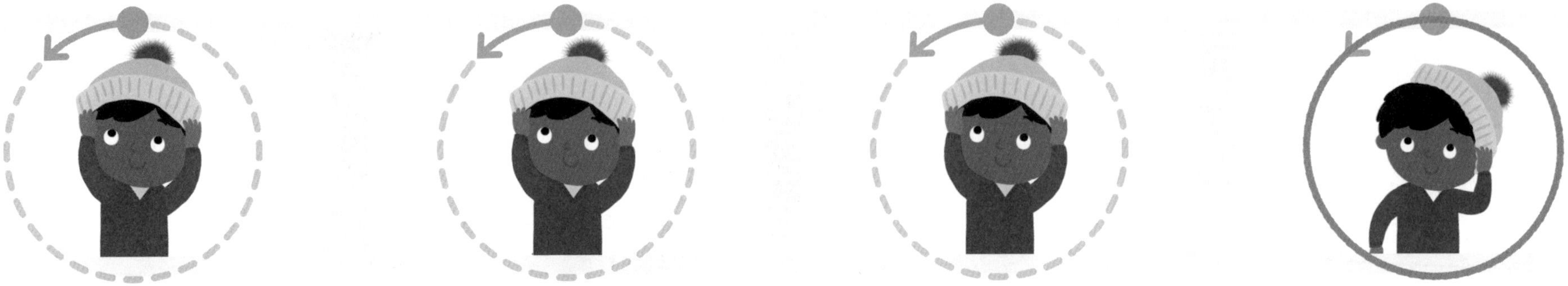

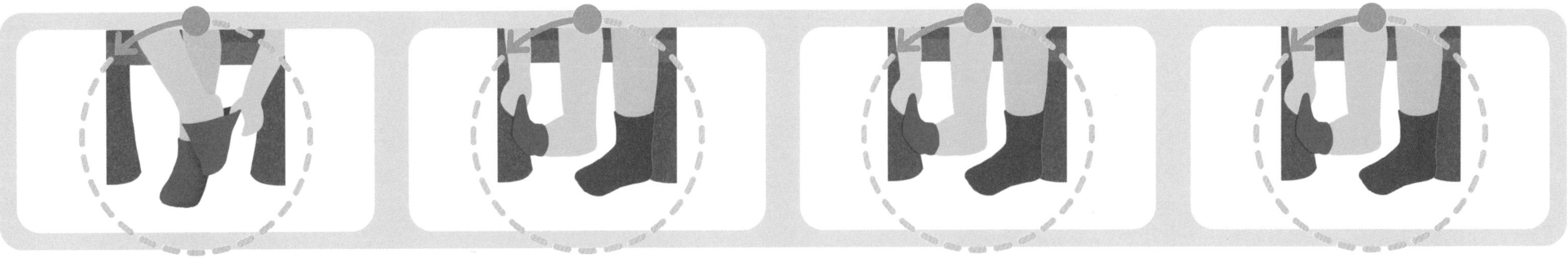

At home Put on a hat, socks, shoes and a jacket. Say.

7 **Language practice:** *(Put on / Take off) your (hat / socks / shoes / jacket).*

56 **Listen again. Look. Find. Trace. Say.**

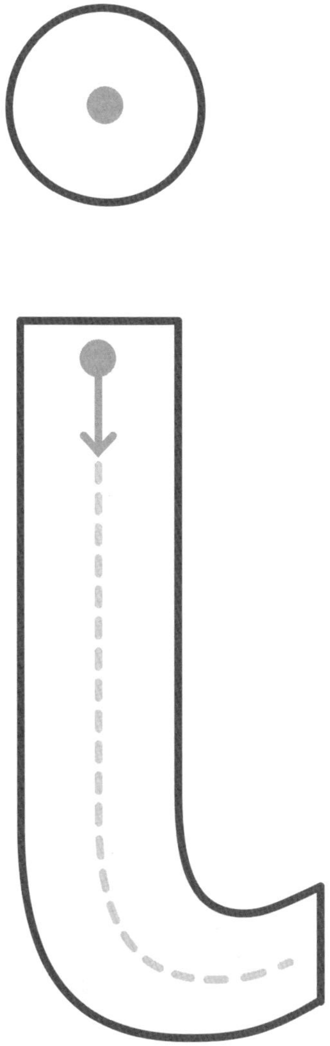

Look. Point. Trace.

Draw. Color. Say.

At home How are you considerate?

Look. Find. Color. Say.

Look. Trace. Say.

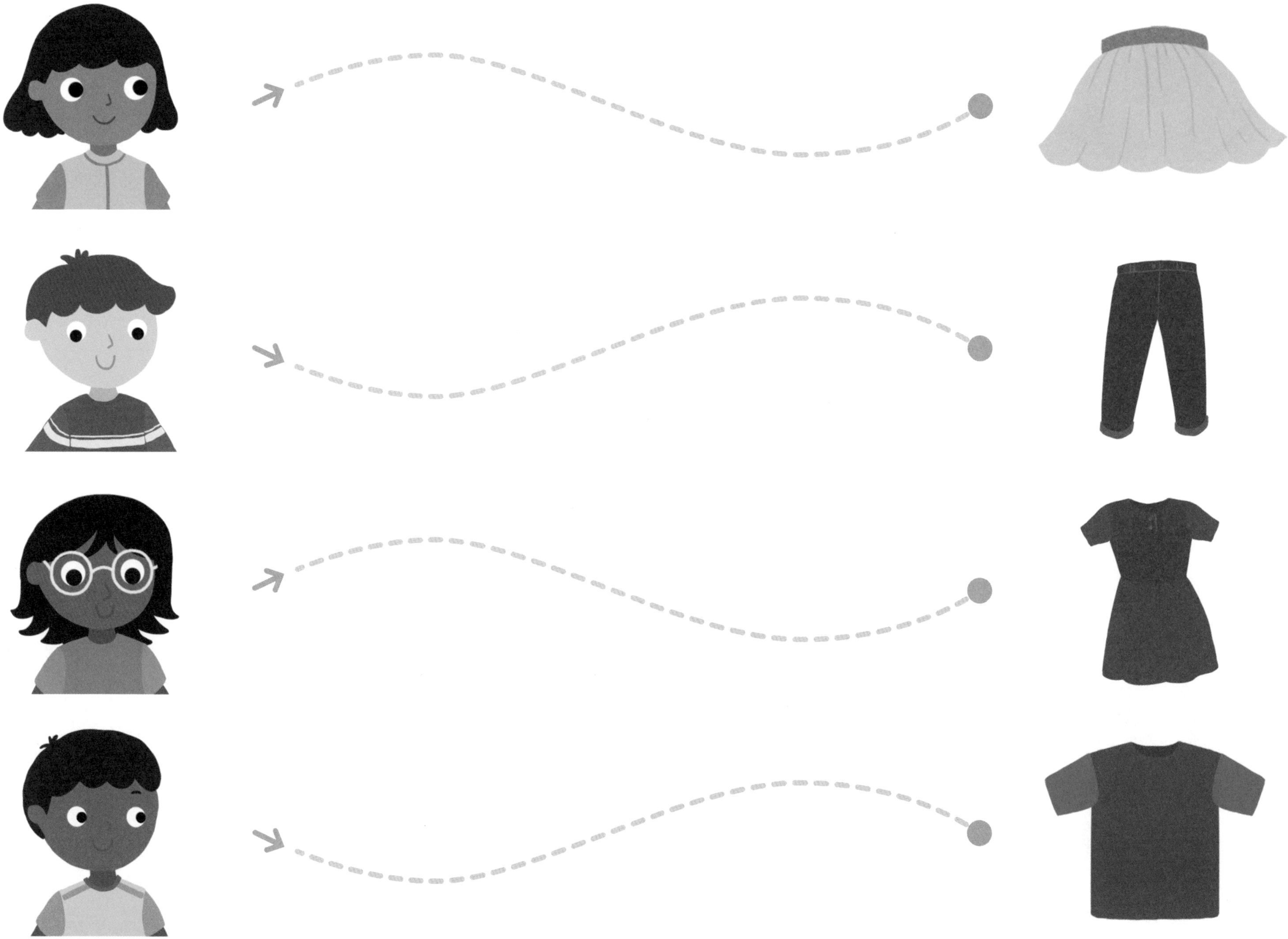

Look. Trace. Say.

At home Find a triangle, a square and a circle.

Look. Find. Color.

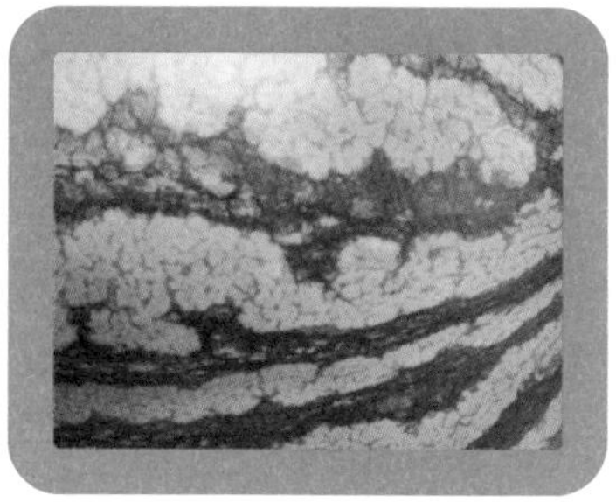

Look. Draw. Say.

7 *(Put on / Take off) your (socks).*

Point. Say. Color.

8 Transportation

61 Listen again. Look. Stick. Point.

Look. Find. Circle. Say.

At home Look outside. Can you see a car, a bus, a bike and a van?

Look. Find. Trace. Say.

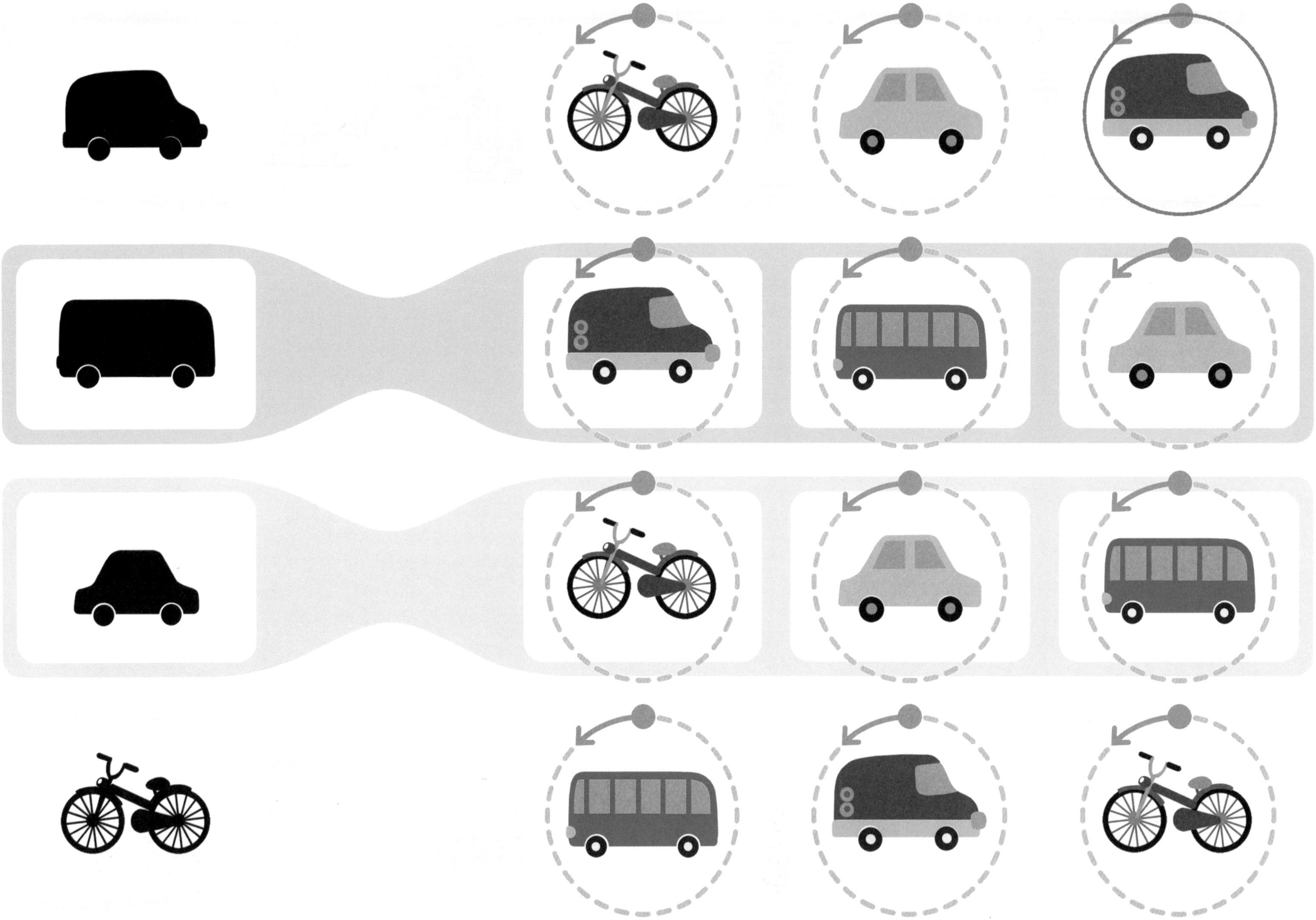

64 **Listen again.** **Look.** **Find.** **Trace.** **Say.**

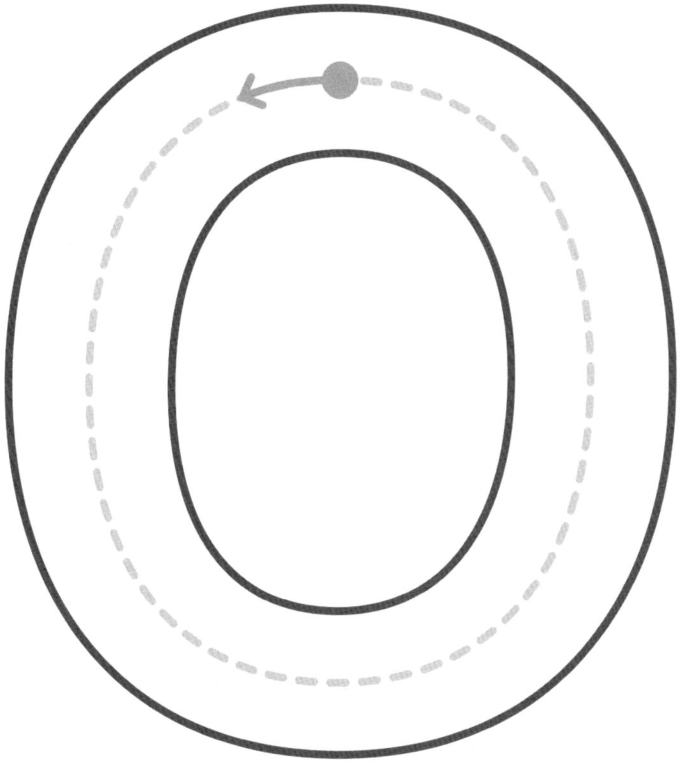

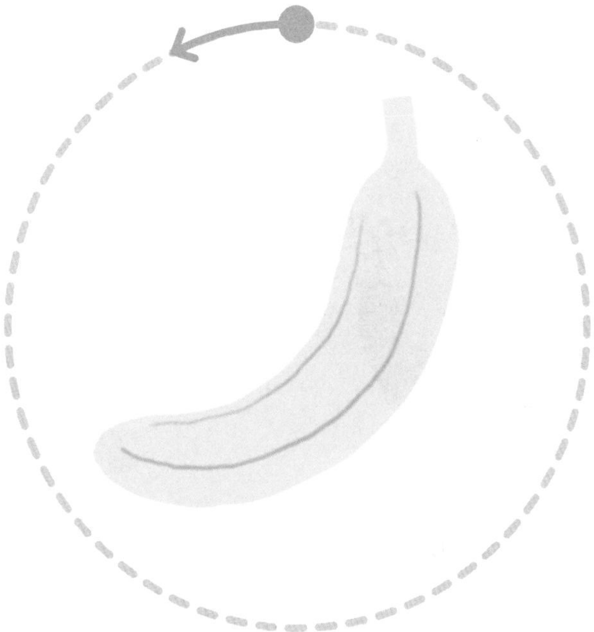

Look. Point. Trace.

Look. Find. Color.

At home

When are you careful?

Look. Color. Say.

Look. Find. Trace. Say.

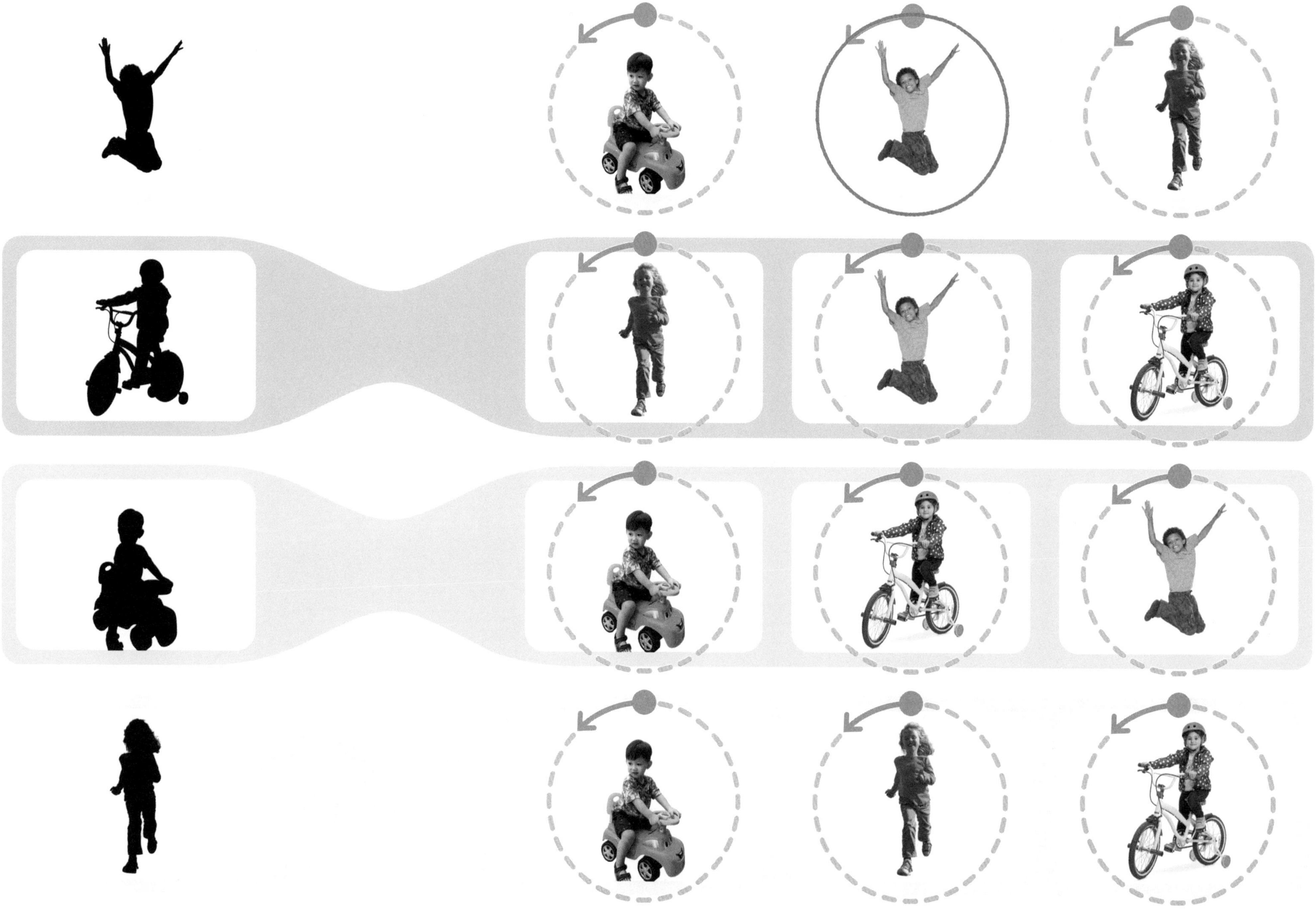

At home Can you jump, ride a bike, drive a car and run?

Language practice: *I can (jump / ride a bike / drive a car / run).*

Look. Count. Trace. Say.

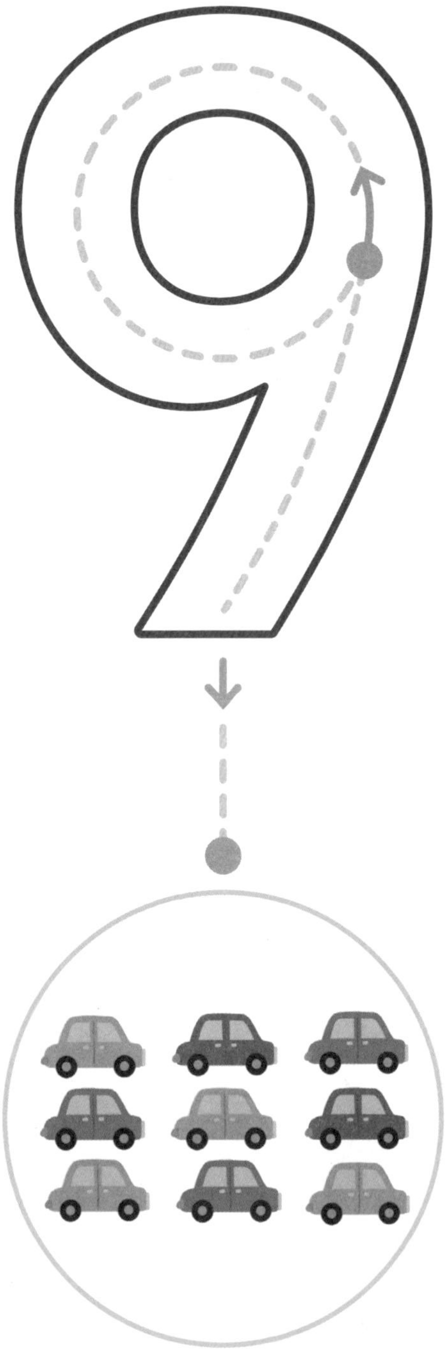

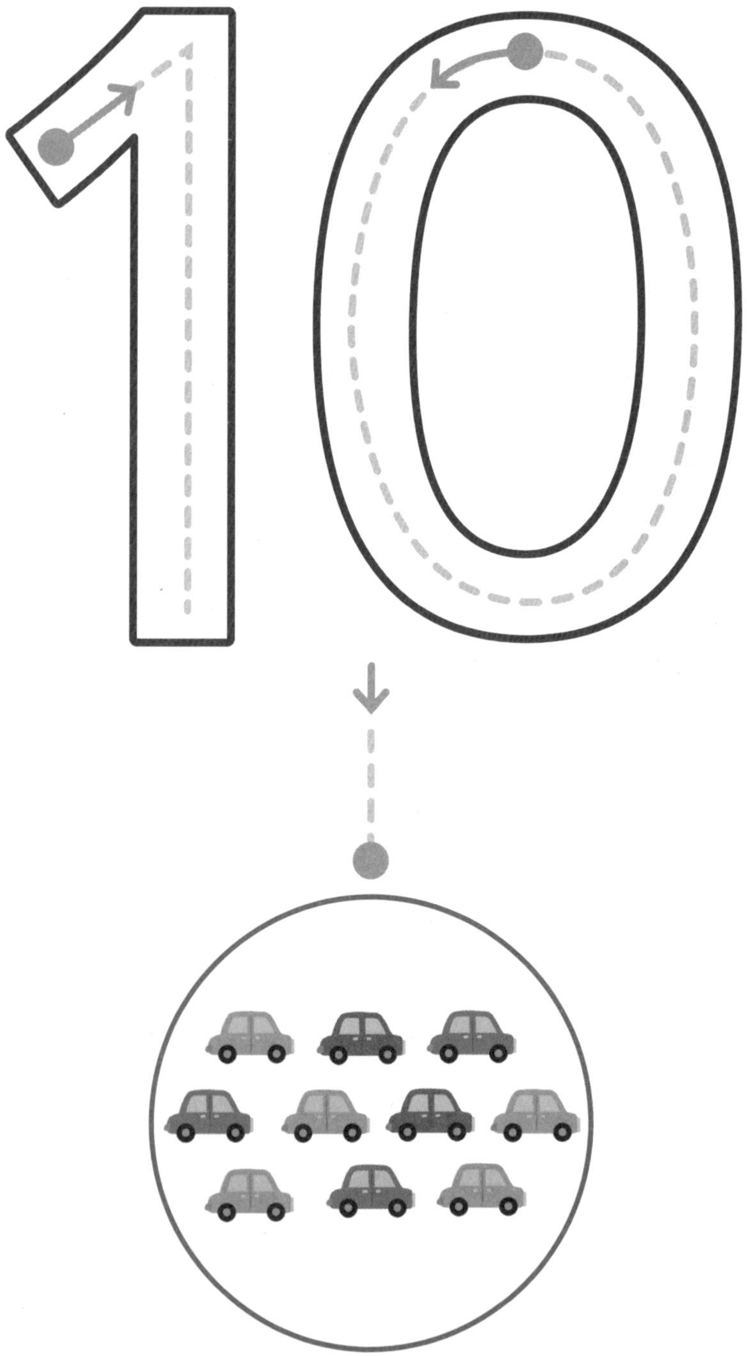

Look. Find. Trace. Say.

Look. Draw. Say.

Point. Say. Color.

I can (drive a car / run / ride a bike / jump).

9 The park

70 **Listen again. Look. Stick. Point.**

Look. Find. Color. Say.

Look. Find. Trace. Say.

9 **Language practice:** *a green tree, a brown frog, a blue bird, a pink flower*

At home Find something pink and something green.

73 **Listen again. Look. Find. Trace. Say.**

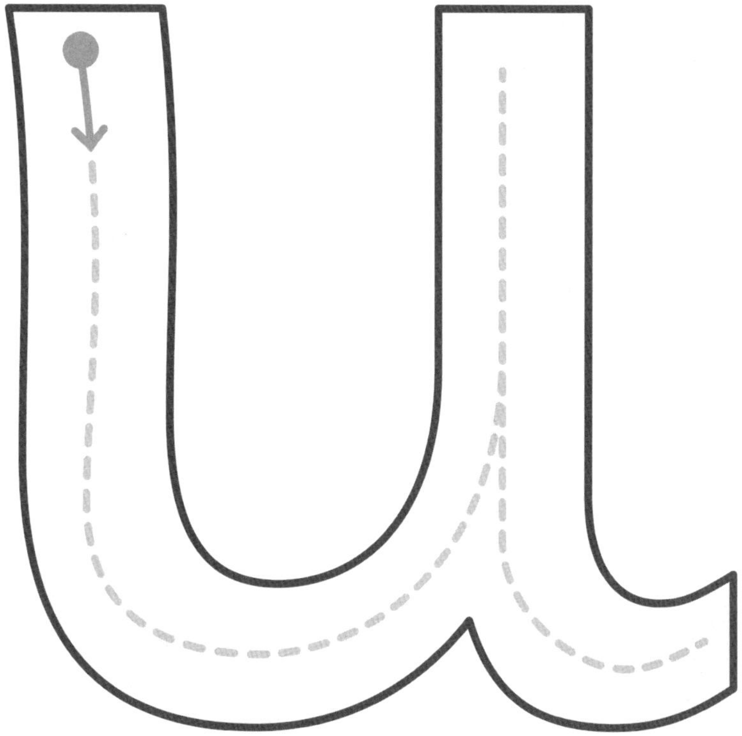

Look. Point. Trace.

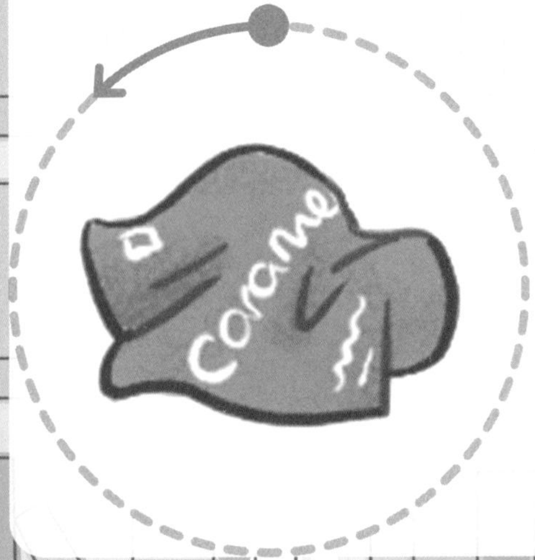

Look. Find. Color.

At home

How do you take care of nature?

Look. Trace. Say.

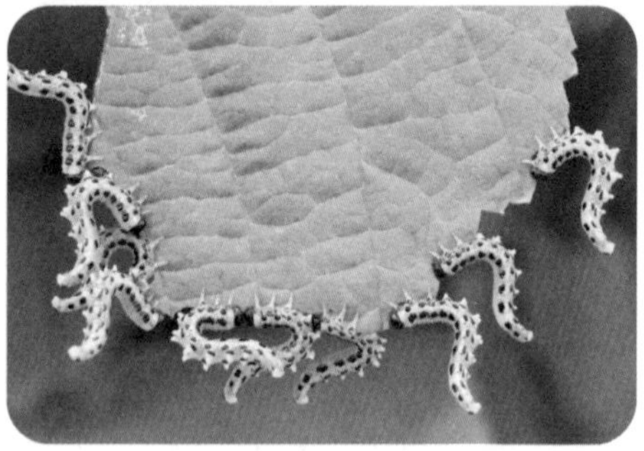

Look. Color. Say.

At home Look outside. Can you find a butterfly, a caterpillar, a worm or a ladybug?

Language practice: *They're (butterflies / caterpillars / worms / ladybugs).*

Look. Count. Trace. Say.

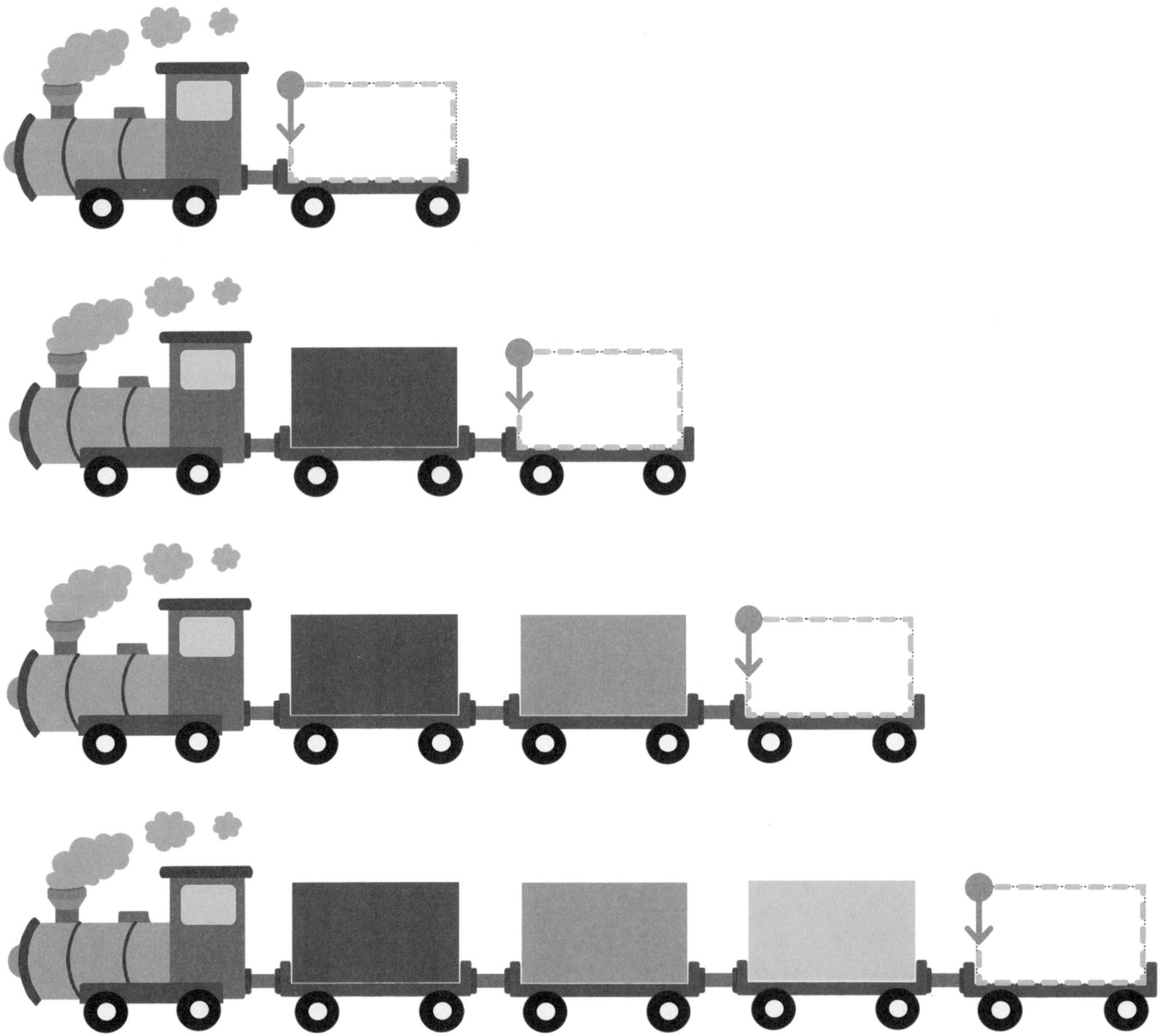

Look. Trace. Color. Say.

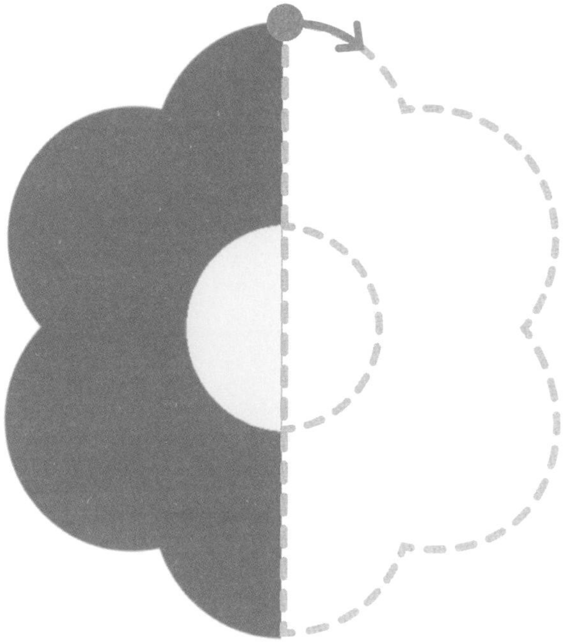

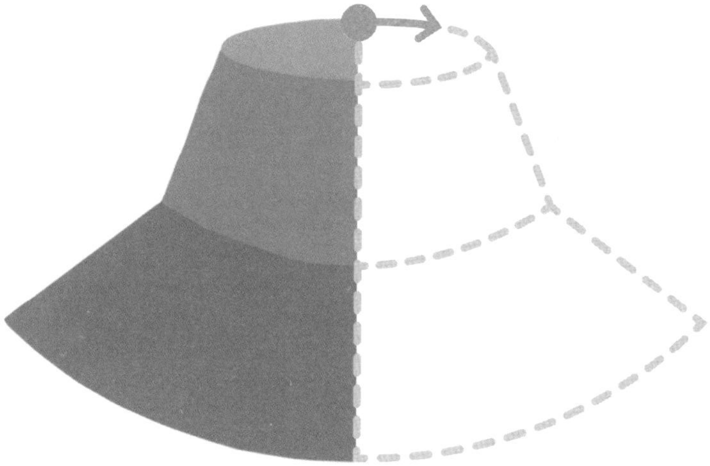

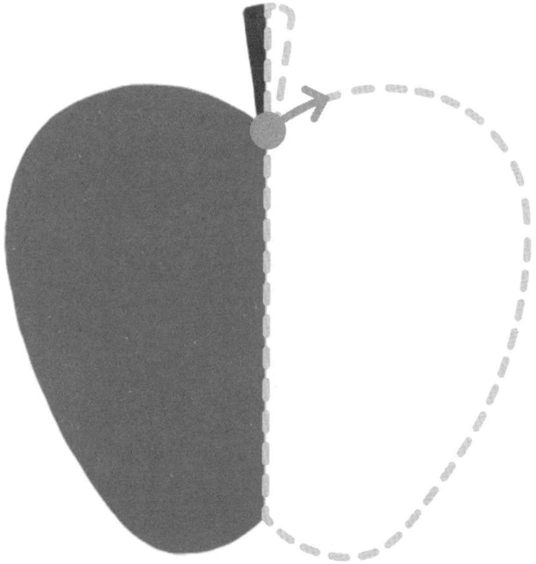

Look. Draw. Say.

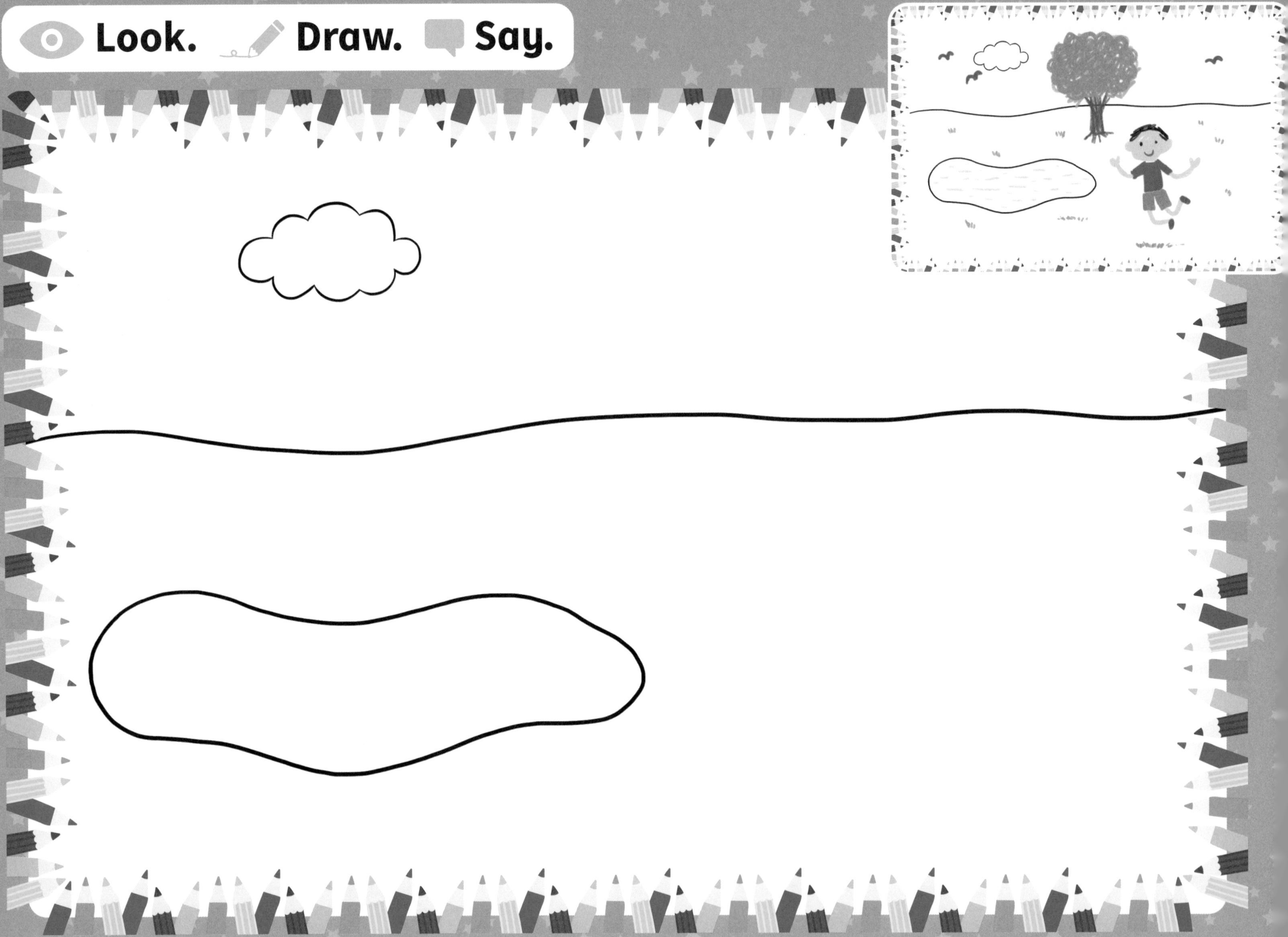

9 *A (green) (tree).*

Point. Say. Color.

They're (butterflies / ladybugs / worms / caterpillars).

Look. Find. Color. Say.

Look. Count. Trace. Say.

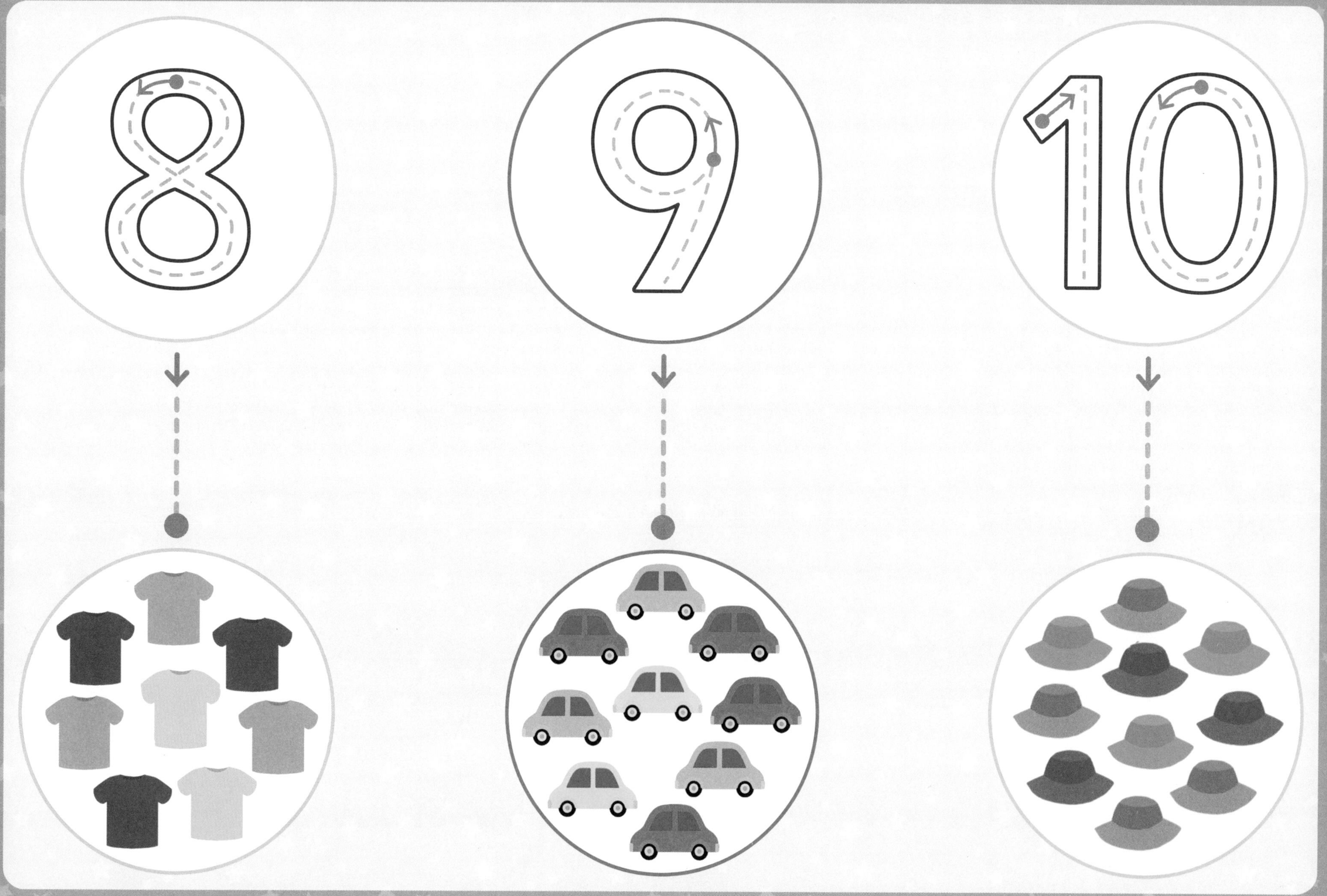

Thanks and Acknowledgements

The publishers and authors would like to thank the following contributors:
Book design and page make-up by Blooberry Design.
Cover design by Blooberry Design.
Freelance editing by Karen Cleveland Marwick and Stephanie Howard.
Editorial project management by Emma Ramírez.
Audio recording and production by Ian Harker.
Original songs and chants by Robert Lee.
Songs and chants production by Jake Carter.

The authors and publishers acknowledge the following sources of copyright material and are grateful for the permissions granted. While every effort has been made, it has not always been possible to identify the sources of all the material used, or to trace all copyright holders. If any omissions are brought to our notice, we will be happy to include the appropriate acknowledgements on reprinting and in the next update to the digital edition, as applicable.

Key: U = Unit.

Photography

All photos are sourced from Getty Images.
U1: Thanasis Zovoilis/Moment; Zero Creatives/Image Source; Liam Norris/Taxi/Getty Images Plus; Mai Vu/iStock/Getty Images Plus; **U2:** monkeybusinessimages/iStock/Getty Images Plus; Jose Luis Pelaez Inc/DigitalVision; BJI/Blue Jean Images; 4x6/E+; JGI/Jamie Grill; Imazins; Mai Vu/iStock/Getty Images Plus; **U3:** Floortje/E+; bbtomas/iStock/Getty Images Plus; Rastko Belic/EyeEm; skodonnell/iStock/Getty Images Plus; Vesnaandjic/iStock/Getty Images Plus; Moyo Studio/E+; Sydney Bourne/Cultura; Mai Vu/iStock/Getty Images Plus; **U4:** Sally Anscombe/DigitalVision; Jose Luis Pelaez Inc/DigitalVision; Camille Tokerud/Stone; images by Tang Ming Tung/Moment; Iliana Mestari/Moment; Victoria Penafiel/Moment/Getty Images Plus; photography by Rick Lowe/Moment; Anna Bizon; didesign021/iStock/Getty Images Plus; Mai Vu/iStock/Getty Images Plus; **U5:** Mike Kemp; imagenavi; Frontdoor Images/Photodisc; Mai Vu/iStock/Getty Images Plus; **U6:** Jessica Peterson; Halfpoint Images/Moment; Helen Davies/iStock/Getty Images Plus; Derick Hudson/iStock/Getty Images Plus; Ron Sutherland/ Photolibrary/Getty Images Plus; jclegg/E+; Kathy Collins/Photographer's Choice RF; Jose Luis Pelaez Inc/DigitalVision; Mai Vu/iStock/Getty Images Plus; **U7:** Jessica Peterson; PhotoAlto/Eric Audras/PhotoAlto Agency RF Collections; Zohaib Hussain; Mai Vu/iStock/Getty Images Plus; **U8:** imagewerks; Tom Merton/OJO Images; Ljupco/iStock/Getty Images Plus; Wong Siewhong/EyeEm; Westend61; amwu/iStock/Getty Images Plus; simonkr/E+; 4x6/iStock/Getty Images Plus; YouraPechkin/iStock/Getty Images Plus; MediaProduction/iStock/Getty Images Plus; technotr/E+; Halfpoint/iStock/Getty Images Plus; Peter Cade/Stone; Mai Vu/iStock/Getty Images Plus; **U9:** Ariel Skelley/DigitalVision; Tetra Images; Petro Perutskyi/500Px Plus; Valengilda/iStock/Getty Images Plus; Flavio Coelho/Moment; Laurie Gresch/EyeEm; mikroman6/Moment; Mik122/iStock/Getty Images Plus;Mai Vu/iStock/Getty Images Plus;JGI/Tom Grill; BartCo/E+.

Illustrations
Amy Zhing; Beatriz Castro; Begoña Corbalán; Isabelle Nichole; Noopur Thakur; Louise Forshaw and Collaborate artists.
Cover illustration by Collaborate Agency.